CONTENTS

The author with Takeo Yamashita

INTRODUCTION

From the southern slopes of Mount Ainslie in the Australian capital, Canberra, the Australian War Memorial dominates the city. A massive tomb-like structure, the Memorial has no counterpart in the world. It serves not only as a solemn monument to the nation's war dead but also as a functional repository for relics of all wars in which Australians have fought and as a vast library for documentary records.

First opened to the public on Armistice Day 1941, the Australian War Memorial began as an idea "conceived on the battlefront, born amid the thunder of guns at Bullecourt ... and raised by the living members of the Australian forces to their fallen mates. Thus, this national collection is unique in that it constitutes not a general museum portraying war, much less glorifying it, but a memorial conceived, founded and, from first to last, worked for by Australia's soldiers, sailors and airmen."

The Memorial has many purely commemorative features including a Roll of Honour of Australian war dead, inscribed on bronze plates, containing 102,000 names and a mosaic consisting of over six million pieces of coloured tesserae weighing 15 tons. Its magnificent library contains 70,000 books; 5000 volumes of bound periodicals; a comprehensive collection of military maps; newspaper and press cuttings; sound recordings; some 240,000 photographic negatives; and about four million feet of cine film exposed by official war cameramen.

Huge exhibition galleries have on display paintings by official war artists; models and dioramas and relics ranging in size from a huge Lancaster bomber to a tiny radio set concealed in a hollowed-out book once used by Australian prisoners of war in Japanese-held territory to receive news broadcasts.

An eighty-foot Japanese midget submarine stands as a mute reminder of one of the most daring naval actions of World War II. The scarred and shattered submarine is actually a composite of the remains of two which were destroyed by Allied action during the midget submarine attack on Sydney Harbour on 31 May 1942.

Inside the War Memorial is a small piece of cloth labelled "body belt" which was worn during the raid by Lieutenant Keiu Matsuo, commander of the midget launched from parent submarine I-22. Careful examination of the bloodstained piece of body belt reveals a multitude of stitches sewn into the cloth, each one of which is tied in a small knot. Also written on the cloth in Japanese characters are six names, one of which is the name of Keiu Matsuo's sister, Mrs Fujie Saeki, who made the belt and presented it to Matsuo in 1939 on his graduation from Naval College as Second Sub-Lieutenant.

The origin of the Japanese custom of presenting a body belt, called Senninbari (people's thousand stitches) is obscure but the purpose was spiritual or semi-religious. It was customary in Japan for every man going to war to be given a Senninbari measuring about one metre long and fifteen centimetres wide. Incorporated in the cloth were one thousand stitches, the first one made by a blood relation of the soldier and the remainder made by 999 other women. The belief was that the soldier would be protected by the power of a thousand women, so it was an expression of heartfelt wish for his safety.

Keiu Matsuo wore his Senninbari for three years and when he died at the age of 26, on the bottom of Sydney Harbour, the belt was wound around his waist.

The existence of Matsuo's body belt in the Australian War Memorial remained unknown to Matsuo's relatives, or to anyone else in Japan, until 1964. It was discovered there by Takeo Yamashita, a former naval petty officer, who had come to Australia to visit an Australian who had befriended him after he had been taken prisoner in the Celebes at the end of the war. Yamashita, then an Inspector of Police in Osaka, who had by this time published his book *The Southern Cross Stars*, was visiting Canberra to present a copy to the Director of the Australian War Memorial, Major J. McGrath.

By a singular coincidence Yamashita, on seeing the body belt, was not only able to explain its significance but also to identify its original owner. Aware that Australia had given the crews of the destroyed midget submarines decent burial with full naval honours and had returned their ashes to Japan even at a desperate stage of the war, Yamashita had come to Australia with feelings of gratitude for such chivalry.

Excited by his discovery, Takeo Yamashita endeavoured to arrange the return of the body belt to the bereaved relatives in Japan. The Board of Trustees of the Australian War Memorial, however, were unable to grant his request as to do so would create a precedent resulting in a possible deluge of similar requests.

As an alternative the Director of the War Memorial arranged for enlarged photographs of Matsuo's former possessions to be sent to his mother, Mrs Matsue Matsuo, together with an explanation why it was considered impracticable to return the Senninbari. In the covering letter the Director added: "You will be aware that the bravery of your son and other members of the crew was so highly appreciated that they were given a military funeral at the time."

On receiving the picture of her son's Senninbari Mrs Matsue Matsuo offered to present it to his former Naval College, the First Technical School of the Japanese Marine Self Defence Force. The Principal of the school gladly accepted the offer and the picture is exhibited in the School hall. The presentation to the School was made by Kiyoi Ageta who commanded the submarine I-22 which launched Matsuo's midget on its mission of death. The tomb of Commander Keiu Matsuo, who had been promoted two ranks after death, lies in a suburb of Yamaga city, his birthplace in Kumamoto Prefecture.

The story of Takeo Yamashita's discovery aroused tremendous interest in Japan and was widely published in newspapers and magazines. The story revived not only the tragic memory of the midget submarine attack on Sydney, but the record of Australia's civilised treatment of the dead crews at the time.

1

On Sunday, 31 May, 1942, Sydney was feeling the first sharp bite of winter. To the east the sea was turbulent and white-capped under a leaden sky and a cutting wind blew from the south-east Australia was at war but for the people of Sydney on that autumn day, danger was a long way to the north.

Some three months earlier bombs had fallen on the Australian mainland for the first time when Vice-Admiral Chuichi Nagumo led a powerful naval force to within 200 miles north of Darwin. Nagumo, who had earlier taken part in the Pearl Harbour attack, turned his four aircraft carriers into the wind on the morning of 19 February and soon afterwards his Zero fighters and Mitsubishi bombers were swarming over Darwin town and harbour.

Swooping on the Royal Australian Air Force station they bombed and strafed hangars, aircraft, oil tanks and dispersal bays. Moving on over the town they dropped fifteen large bombs which demolished the post office and killed its occupants and damaged homes and buildings. Within half an hour they had gone leaving 250 dead and six ships sunk in the harbour.

During the previous month the Japanese had established themselves in New Britain, the Solomons and on the north coast of New Guinea. Less than three weeks previously they had attempted to invade Port Moresby but their plans had been frustrated by the outcome of the Battle of the Coral Sea.

Two days before 31 May, the National Emergency Service had issued two standby warnings and unidentified aircraft had been reported over the Sydney and Newcastle areas, but otherwise a peacetime tempo prevailed in the harbour city.

Unknown to Sydney citizens enjoying their Sunday relaxation, however, five large ocean going Japanese submarines were lying in wait all that day less than ten miles from Sydney Harbour Heads.

The submarines were units of the Sydney Attack Group under the command of Captain Hankyu Sasaki. The attacking force consisted of two submarine companies, the 3rd Company composed of submarines I-21, I 22 and I-24 directly controlled by Captain Sasaki and the 14th Company with I-27 and I-29 under the command of Captain Katsuta. Katsuta's third submarine, I-28, had been sunk south of Truk by an American submarine a fortnight previously.

Two of the huge submarines I-21 and I-29 were seaplane carriers and clamped on the decks of the other three were two-men submarines destined that night for targets inside the harbour itself. In the late afternoon Commander Kiyoi Ageta, captain of I-22, brought his submarine to the surface and peered through his periscope across the choppy sea. The coast was clear. So far so good.

Lieutenant Keiu Matsuo, who had been chosen to command the midget submarine clamped on I-22's deck, was then brought into the final discussion.

"It'll be quite a job to attack such a long and complicated harbour as Sydney," Commander Ageta said. "I'd like to get a bit closer to the Heads, but it's not worth running the risk from the indicator loops they have fixed there."

"Don't worry, Captain," Matsuo said cheerfully. "Since we left Truk ten days ago I've spent most of my time over the charts of Sydney Harbour. I know every nook and cranny of it."

The attack had been planned to take advantage of the full moon and a complete program from start to recovery of the midgets had been carefully worked out.

A line had been drawn on the chart between the projecting points of North and South Heads at the entrance to Port Jackson channel. From the centre of that line a semi-circle was drawn to the east with a radius of twenty miles. The semi-circle was then divided into three equal sectors which became the positions of I-27, I-22 and I-24 from north to south respectively. I-29 and I-21 were to take up positions outside the semi-circle, the former in the north and the latter in the south. From these positions the parent submarines were to launch their midgets underwater.

After the attack the midgets were to sail to a rendezvous twenty miles south of the centre of the channel entrance where the parent submarines would be waiting for them on the surface. The plan was for the submarines to lie in two lines, I-24, I-22 and I-27 from west to east at intervals of about two miles in one line and I-21 and I-29 likewise in a second line about three miles south of the first.

After recovering the crews it was proposed to sink the midgets.

The order of invasion was for I-27's midget to pass the Heads one hour after sunset, to be followed at thirty-minute intervals by I-24's midget and I-22's midget.

While Matsuo talked to his captain at the periscope housing he was joined by his friend and room-mate First Sub-Lieutenant Muniaki Fujisawa who was in charge of I-22's torpedoes. Fujisawa had taken special care of Matsuo during the voyage from Truk and had earlier cut his friend's hair and shaved him as a farewell gesture.

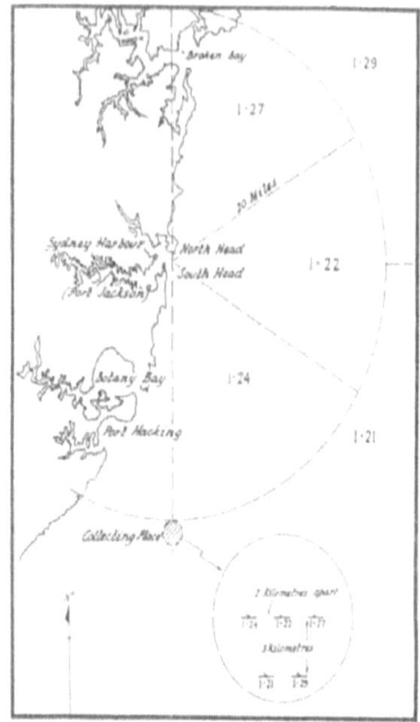

A reproduction of the Japanese plan to attack Sydney Harbour and vital coastal shipping lanes.

He had confidence in Matsuo's capability but he knew from the midget submarine disasters at Pearl Harbour what the chances of survival were. Also standing by, but saying nothing, was the Chief Engineer, Lieutenant Terashita, who had come to take a photograph of Matsuo before he set out on his mission.

As darkness closed in around the periscope an atmosphere of tenseness developed in the confined space of the submarine. They knew that the time had come. Matsuo, clad in fresh underwear and his uniform sprayed with perfume, was calm.

Suddenly Commander Ageta's voice broke the silence.

"Lieutenant Matsuo and Petty Officer Tsuzuku. Are you ready?"

"Yes, sir. We are all ready," Matsuo answered.

"Good luck," Ageta said. "We'll pick you up at the appointed place. Be sure to come back, we'll be waiting."

"Thank you, sir. And thank you for your kind attention. The best of luck and good fighting to I-22!"

Through the voice tube Matsuo then made a short address to all of his crew mates elsewhere in the submarine.

"My comrades, I am happy to tell you that at last I am going to attack Sydney. I think I owe much to your help for this day and I would like to thank you all. Good-bye."

With a dagger in his right hand he then climbed through the connecting hatch which, like a stubby umbilical cord, linked the midget submarine to its parent. The dagger had been presented to him in a purple sack by his father. Petty Officer Tsuzuku followed him through the narrow iron connecting hatch and the two men were sealed off from the mother submarine.

About an hour after sunset Commander Ageta gave the order for the mission to begin.

"Start!"

Ageta's voice was unnaturally loud and his eyes were shut as though in prayer.

The midget's binding clamps were unloosed and the telephone cord was cut. I-22 submerged and with a slight shock the arrow was shot from the bow. The midget was floating free and on its way.

The moon was full as Lieutenant Matsuo set his midget's propellers in motion and moved off after the other two midgets from I-27 and I-24.

Right: Lieutenant Keiu Matsuo, commander of I-22's midget submarine in the raid on Sydney Harbour.

Above: Petty Officer Tsuzuku, Matsuo's fellow crew member.

"Midget has started: Direction 275 degrees. Sensitivity five."

I-22's microphones picked up the report from Lieutenant Matsuo and Sugimoto, the parent submarine's navigator, charted the midget's progress. The diminishing sound of propellers recorded by the microphones indicated that the attack was off to a good start.

After dusk on Sunday the lights of Sydney came on as usual. The ocean beaches of Dee Why, Harbord, Manly and Bondi formed a dark eastern edge to the brightly lit city, which went about its holiday business in much the same way as it had done before the Pacific war started.

The tide was coming in and commercial shipping conditions in the harbour were normal. Three American warships including the USS *Chicago* were at anchor and other craft included the Netherlands submarine K9, HMAS *Canberra* and five other Australian warships.

On HMAS *Kuttabul*, a former ferry steamer in use as a naval depot ship, a group of ratings had finished their evening meal. Some were lounging on deck, idly looking across Garden Island, alongside which the ship was moored.

In the I-22, seven miles off the Heads, Commander Ageta anxiously monitored messages from his departed midget.

"Sensitivity Two . . . Sensitivity One."

"Sensitivity zero."

"No sensitivity."

After the last report had been repeated several times the captain suddenly shouted.

"Blow main tank!"

Slowly I-22 broke the surface and her huge outline was revealed in the pale light of a full moon. After strong winds over the previous few days the sea was calm and glimmering like a dark wet mirror. The lighthouse on South Head blinked normally and even the lights on ships anchored in the harbour were clearly visible.

The captain breathed a sigh of relief. Everything about Sydney was normal, while silently and steadily the midget offspring of I-22, I-24 and I-27 were moving towards the peaceful, unsuspecting harbour.

Inside the harbour the Burns Philp Ltd. cargo ship *Mangola* was being readied for sea at her berth in Walsh Bay. Bernard Murphy, fourth engineer came aboard about 7.30 p.m. and prepared to take over the 8 p.m. to midnight watch. The ship was scheduled to leave before 10 p.m. bound for Newcastle. While Murphy was busy in the *Mangola's* engine room James Cargill, a Maritime Services Board watchman, was also on duty, near the submarine boom defences at the harbour entrance.

At about 8.15 p.m. Cargill thought he saw something pass through one of the gaps in the boom net defences and rowed across to the centre portion of the nets, near the Western Gate, to investigate. He saw what appeared to be two oxygen bottles floating just below the surface and decided they belonged either to a mine or a submarine. Rowing back to his post Cargill reported his suspicious discovery to Lieutenant H. C. Eyers who was in command of the naval patrol boat HMAS *Yarroma*.

Meanwhile the *Mangola* with the Sydney pilot aboard was proceeding down the harbour towards the Heads as she had done on hundreds of previous occasions. In the engine room Engineer Murphy answered the telegraph and watched steam pressure, while his colleague Jock Williamson handled the controls. Completely occupied with their work both men were anxious to reach the boom, drop the pilot and make the open sea when they would be able to knock off and get some sleep.

Suddenly the telegraph rang, "stop", then "full astern", then again "stop-". After a few minutes they heard the anchor go down.

"Well, that's the quickest bloody trip we've ever done to Newcastle," Williamson remarked.

Murphy grinned but before he could reply orders came from the bridge for steam to be kept handy to move at short notice.

"Bloody funny," Murphy said. "A man expects this sort of thing around Moresby. I've never struck it before in Sydney Harbour. What's wrong with the dopey galahs!"

Williamson wiped his hands on some cotton waste. "Well, I'm going for some shut-eye. I'm on from four to eight in the morning and it looks like we're going to sit here indefinitely." With that remark he went up on deck. Shortly afterwards Murphy made his way to the freezer flat between decks and peered through the port hole.

Sydney's lights were still burning brightly, but an armed naval trawler with steel helmeted gun crews at the alert was circling the ship.

What a time to pick for a dummy run, Murphy thought, and why pick us to practice on.

He returned to the engine room and soon afterwards the Chief Engineer came down.

"The pilot launch has taken the pilot off, Murph," he said. "Believe it or not the boat crew reckon there's a couple of subs loose in the harbour."

"What a lot of bull," Murphy snorted. "More likely some smart idiot's mistaken a floating beer-bottle for a periscope. If there are subs they'd be Yanks for sure."

His words were cut short by a sudden succession of explosions and gunfire.

Out at sea the mother submarines were dark silent shapes breaking the moonlit surface of the sea.

"Ha, the surprise has succeeded," Commander Ageta beamed to Lieutenant Sugimoto, standing beside him in the conning tower of I-22. The scheduled time for the attack was almost nigh.

Suddenly all lights in Sydney Harbour went out. At the same time the night sky was lit up by hundreds of probing searchlights. There was a shout of joy in I-22's conning tower.

"The Australians think it's an air raid. We've really surprised them."

After a long time the searchlights went out and again Sydney was in darkness.

"Both engines. Full speed ahead!"

"Starboard the helm to the maximum."

I-22 moved towards the place appointed for picking up her midget where she was joined by I-24 and I-27. Previously the submarines had remained half-submerged with only their conning towers protruding from the sea. Now, at great risk to themselves, they surfaced so that the returning midgets might find them easily. All night they waited but there was no sign of the midgets.

This was the first Japanese attempt to bring the war to southern Australia but the method by which it was carried out had its origin in British World War I experiments carried out by Commander Godfrey Herbert, a submarine and Q-boat expert. Herbert had invented a one-man submarine-torpedo for launching from a parent ship. His proposal was considered by the British Admiralty but eventually rejected.

The idea of midget submarines, however, was taken up again by the Japanese after World War 1 and, in 1932, was established as a subject for serious study.

The daring raid on Sydney Harbour was the culmination of twenty years' research and practical experiment.

2

The arrival of Commodore Perry's fleet in Yokohama Bay, in 1853, marked the end of Japan's isolation from world affairs and the following half century witnessed her astonishing transition from an ancient nation to a modern world power.

One of the most remarkable developments during this period was the creation of a Japanese navy modelled on the British navy. Japan sent her naval cadets and students to England for training and from England Japan bought the first of her warships. With English help and direction, Japanese naval power grew so quickly that by 1904 Japan was able to defeat Russia and take over the Russian base at Port Arthur, together with extensive Russian rights in south Manchuria.

The core of Japanese naval development was the Naval College, founded in 1888, on the island of Edashima opposite Kure naval port. Kure in time became one of Japan's three great naval ports and arsenals. Surrounded on three sides by high mountains, it became a centre for naval research and construction and by the outbreak of World War II was producing half of the fighting capacity of Japan's navy. At Kure the great battleship *Yamato* was built and furnished with guns and ammunition and the oxygen torpedo was developed into one of the most efficient weapons in the naval armoury.

While Kure's workshops, docks and factories turned out the machinery of war the nearby Naval College moulded the men who were to operate it. From its early beginnings the College quickly acquired a reputation for thorough training and strict discipline and, although its primary aim was the teaching of tactics and strategy, its graduates were expected to emerge as educated gentlemen.

Inflexible rules governed the lives of naval cadets in the College. For example, when ascending a staircase, they had to run up the steps two at a time however tired they might be. Descending, they were compelled to go slowly, step by step, no matter how pressed for time they might be. Those who could not swim were thrown into the sea and learned in the most natural and direct way possible.

Punishments for any breach of the rules or code of behaviour were extremely severe and at the close of each day students were required to shut their eyes and reflect on the following questions:

Did I not do anything against faith?

Did I not hesitate in doing anything good and correct?

Did I not find myself in drooping spirits?

Did I not spare my efforts?

Was I not lazy?

It was a tough school and one which moulded tough fighting men.

Around 1932, one of the subjects set for study at the College was the feasibility of midget submarines and their potential uses. Experiments began and, between 1938 and 1940, were intensified until, in April 1941, the midget submarine was admitted as a useable arm of the Japanese navy.

The midget which had been developed was seventy-eight feet long, six feet in diameter, with a displacement of forty-six tons. Powered by a secondary battery it had a maximum speed of nineteen knots and could cruise for eighty miles at six knots or sixteen miles at nineteen knots. It was fitted with a conning tower, gyro-compass and two torpedo tubes. It was possible to submerge to 330 feet. The midget was designed to be manned by a crew of two men.

The first trials of the midget submarine were carried out at the small fishing village of Mizukue in the middle of Sada Cape, a long narrow headland of Shikoku projecting into the Bungo Channel entrance of the Seto Inland Sea.

Villagers stared at the strange craft which suddenly appeared in the Bungo Channel and wondered what the young naval officers from Kure Base were doing with it.

The officers, in fact, were becoming conversant with every aspect of its control and management, particularly with the firing of its torpedoes. Submerged, the midget could travel at the remarkably fast speed of nineteen knots, a performance required in the role for which it had been initially designed.

Originally the midget had been intended for use in fleet carriers against similar enemy vessels. In this case it was to have been carried in a large specially adapted surface vessel and discharged on rails from the rear deck when the ship neared the target area. Once in the water the midget would approach enemy capital ships at high speed and fire its two eighteen-inch oxygen torpedoes.

Two ships, the *Chiyoda* and *Chitose*, were specially built, in the guise of sea plane carriers, to carry midget submarines and their call signs on naval radio were reported as seaplane carriers. So secret was the manoeuvre that even senior naval officers had no idea that the ships were linked with midget submarines.

A number of flaws in the reasoning behind this procedure, however, soon became apparent. A submerged midget could not travel more than eighty miles at a speed of six knots. If it increased speed to nineteen knots just before the attack the cruising range of eighty miles became less than forty miles. Taking these factors into account it was decided that the carrier vessel would have to carry the midget to within thirty miles of the target area. It was considered doubtful if this would be wise, even if the carrier ships could match the high speed to the vicinity of enemy warships.

After much deliberation the idea of using midget submarines in fleet-against-fleet operations was abandoned and consideration was next given to the possibility of using them to attack shipping anchored inside harbours. The main obstacle presented by this plan was the difficulty in recovering midgets after attacks.

In a battle at sea, midgets could travel a reasonable distance submerged before surfacing to rejoin the carrier vessel. Returning from a harbour attack it was thought doubtful whether midgets could cover their traces and safely rejoin a vessel on the surface. In either case it was planned to sink the midgets after the crews had been recovered.

The next idea to be studied was the transport of midgets by submarine. Naval experts finally agreed that this was the answer to all their problems. Parent submarines could carry the midgets, submerged, to the very mouths of enemy harbours. An ingenious concept! Surfacing at night they could release them almost in sight of their targets.

Throughout the various changes of plans and strategy for the employment of midget submarines there was never any suggestion that they be regarded as suicide craft. In fact, the Chief Commander of the combined fleet, Admiral Isoroku Yamamoto, continued to withhold approval of midget submarine operations until it could be demonstrated that crews could be recovered.

Finally a scheme was evolved whereby midget submarines would be equipped with wireless transmitters and receivers so that they could maintain constant communication with the midget tenders. Believing that this would ensure safe recovery of midget crews Admiral Yamamoto in April 1941 approved the formation of special midget submarine units.

Accordingly, twelve young officers, three warrant officers and twelve petty officers were selected to make up crews for the first operational midget submarines.

The United States heavy cruiser _Chicago_, at anchor in Sydney Harbour on the day of the attack.

The crew of the _Chiyoda_, originally built in the guise of a sea plane tender to carry and launch midget submarines.

All had to be bachelors and each submarine was to be manned by two men — the officer to be responsible for direction, speed, wireless communication and target calculations. The accompanying petty officer was required to look after steering, air-conditioning, depth, battery operation and the firing of torpedoes.

Exceptional intelligence and adaptability were needed in the men who manned submarines. The interior of the large I-class submarines was so complicated that each of the eighty men crew had to be an honours graduate from the Naval Submarine Crew Training School. Midget submarines were equally complex, although on a much smaller scale, but all operations had to be carried out by only the two men.

Three of the men selected for the midget submarine service, in 1941, Keiu Matsuo, Kenshi Chuma and Sabura Akieda, had graduated from the 66th term of the Kure Naval College in September 1938. They had served on training ships and with the combined fleet, became Second Sub-Lieutenants in June 1939, and First Lieutenants in November 1940.

Keiu Matsuo was the son of an elementary school headmaster at

Yamaga in Kumamoto Prefecture. After completing his compulsory primary schooling Keiu Matsuo entered Kamoto Prefectural high school where he distinguished himself as a scholar and sportsman.

While at high school he formed the habit, along with other students, of paying homage to a Shrine about eight miles away. The Shrine belonged to the clan of Kikuchi which had left many names famous in the military history of the province. Here the seed was sown which was later to bear fruit in Matsuo's gallantry in Sydney Harbour.

Although a serious student, Matsuo's strong will and fixed convictions often led him into scrapes and trouble. One incident, in which he narrowly avoided clashing with the school authorities, concerned his High School brass band. The band, which was a very good one, had been invited to perform on the local radio station. After this, its members became somewhat conceited and boastful, so much so that they incurred the disapproval of Keiu Matsuo, who decided to puncture their self esteem. With some of his friends Matsuo worked out a drastic method of chastising the band — by lynching its members. The plot, however, leaked out and Matsuo was persuaded by his teacher to settle for methods less violent.

After graduation from High School, Matsuo entered the Naval College at Kure where his career as a naval officer soon became assured. There were times throughout his cadet training, however, when his reckless spirit asserted itself. One occasion was when he had failed to qualify for transfer to the Flying Corps. Leaving his destroyer he disappeared for three days. At the end of that time he sent a letter from a bar informing his shipmates that he had spent all his money. His friends passed around the hat and finally brought him back to his ship.

Another young man selected for midget submarine training was Masas Tsuzuku, later to become Keiu Matsuo's fellow crew member in I-22's midget submarine raid on Sydney Harbour. Tsuzuku was the son of poor farmers in the mountains of Gifu Prefecture and, as a boy, had been unable to travel the long distance to the nearest school. Instead, his daily job was burning charcoal. At night, however, he studied books borrowed from a neighbour by his mother, using the light of a metal hand lamp.

"You are poor," his mother would tell him, "but our ancestor was a Samurai and you have Samurai blood in your veins."

At the age of eighteen years Tsuzuku made up his mind to become a naval cadet but, through lack of proper education, he failed the examination.

He tried again the following year and, this time, was successful. Later, after graduating from the Torpedo and Submarine schools, he joined the specially picked band of midget submariners.

With the selection of specific crews the employment of midget submarines in action became preordained. Agreement had been reached that harbours were to be the exclusive targets for midgets and consequently study was directed towards overcoming or evading the defences generally encountered in such places. There was no way by which indicator loops could be avoided but the Japanese navy experts insisted that something could be done about anti-submarine nets — by passing over or under them, or else cutting through them.

As a result the completed midget submarine was fitted with a saw tooth cutter fixed between the conning tower and the bow. At this stage the midget submarine was officially called a "special shed pipe" in order to conceal its true identity and purposes.

So successfully was the secret kept that not even Captain Iura, who was to serve as a submarine staff officer at Pearl Harbour and later to take charge of strategy for the Sydney Harbour and Diego Suarez midget submarine attacks, knew what was going on.

A few naval officers had noticed the abnormally large cranes on the *Chiyoda* but the deception was maintained until September 1941 when plans were disclosed to chief staff officers and commanders of fleets and squadrons at the Tokyo Naval College.

While Matsuo and Tsuzuku neared completion of their training, Japan herself was preparing a daring and widespread offensive behind a barrier of even greater stealth. By the middle of August 1941, a blueprint for war submitted by the Japanese Planning Board had been provisionally adopted by the High Command.

The plan called for simultaneous operations against the Philippines and Malaya and a subsequent southward drive against Java from both east and west.

In September 1941, a large scale exercise was carried out under the supervision of Admiral Yamamoto, Commander-in-Chief of the combined fleet. The exercise provided for a naval operation to gain command of the sea in the Western Pacific, leading to capture of American, British and Dutch areas in the southern region and a surprise attack on Hawaii. The study and exercise for a surprise attack on Hawaii, which had been under consideration since the previous January, was carried out in the strictest secrecy.

One of the select band of naval officers who shared in the stealthy preparations for Pearl Harbour was Lieutenant Matsuo. Then a Sub-Lieutenant, he was assigned to special espionage duty in Hawaii and, on 13 October 1941, visited Pearl Harbour in the disguise of a seaman of the North American Line. While in Pearl Harbour he ascertained the types of equipment in use and the location of key installations.

On 23rd October 1941, a submarine squadron, including I-22, was on exercises practising to break into a harbour supposedly guarded by enemy destroyers. Suddenly I-22 received orders to return to Kure and lie alongside the pier of the Naval Arsenal.

When I-22 tied up at the pier, her crew was astonished to see a team of workmen come aboard and begin demolishing the rear deck. The work continued all night and well into the following morning. I-22's crew members were even more perplexed when the arsenal workers said that they themselves did not know why they were making such preparations. It was obvious, however, that the purpose of new fittings on I-22's deck was to embark something very big.

On 1 November, four recent graduates of the Submarine School came aboard. Two of them, Lieutenant Iwasa and Warrant Officer Sasaki, were midget submarine crew members and the other two were petty officers trained in the equipment of midget submarines. Finally, while the crew of I-22 was below, arsenal workers loaded the midget on the big submarine's deck.

First Lieutenant Matsuo came aboard and on 6 November I-22 left Kure to carry out midget launching exercises. No one, apart from the Captain, Matsuo and the two midget submarine crewmen, knew that the object clamped on deck was indeed a midget submarine. Most of them thought it was a tank.

After leaving Kure, I-22 spent over a week on exercises with the new weapon which was handled exclusively by arsenal workers and the special crew members who had come on board. These men practised unbinding and launching the midget while I-22 played her part in practice recoveries. Even at this stage the general submarine crew members were not sure what the strange weapon was or what its purpose might be.

On 15 November I-22 returned to Kure and took on water and rations for

100 days — torpedoes and ammunition having been loaded six weeks earlier. During the following two days the crew rested and wrote letters but these were strictly censored, particularly in regard to any mention as to where the submarine was located at the time.

Meanwhile, from 10 November, units of the Japanese combined fleet had been leaving home ports one after another, bound for a rendezvous at Hitocup Harbour in Etorofu of the Kurile Islands. The submarine division with the midgets, however, took a different course.

On 17 November, the last conference on the midget submarine attack plan was held at Kure Naval Post. It was attended by the commandant of the division, captains of submarines and officers allocated to man midget submarines. First Sub-Lieutenant Matsuo was also in attendance to pass on information he had gathered on Pearl Harbour's defences during his previous intelligence mission. The conference agreed that a midget attack on Pearl Harbour was feasible and on the following day five submarines assigned for the attack left Kure.

On the way I-22 stopped at Kamegakubi, the midget submarine base, and embarked a midget. Then, for the first time the crew was told what it was and informed of its purpose. After the midget had been equipped and I-22 got under way again, Captain Ageta told his men that their destination was Hawaii.

The five huge I-class midget carrying submarines, each displacing over 2000 tons, were attached to the third flotilla of the First Submarine squadron under the command of Captain Hankyu Sasaki.

Parent submarine captains and midget crews assigned to carry out the Pearl Harbour mission were:

SUBMARINE	CAPTAIN	MIDGET CREW
I-16	Commander Kaoru Yamada	First Sub-Lieutenant Masaji Yokayama Second Petty Officer Sadashi Ueda
I-18	Commander Kiyonori Ohtani	First Sub-Lieutenant Shigeru Furuno First Petty Officer Kunhan Yokoyama
I-20	Commander Takashi Yamada	Second Sub-Lieutenant Akira Hiroo Second Petty Officer Yoshio Katayama
I-22	Commander Kiyoi Ageta	Lieutenant Naoji Iwasa First Petty Officer Naokichi Sasaki
I-24	Commander Hiroshi Hanafusa	First Sub-Lieutenant Kazuo Sakamaki Second Petty Officer Kiyoshi Inagaki

Above left: Captain Hankyu Sasaki, overall commander of the midget submarine raids on Pearl Harbour and Sydney. Above right: First Sub-Lieutenant Ban, commander of I-24's midget which fired the torpedo that sank HMAS *Kuttabul* in the raid on Sydney Harbour.

Bottom: Members of midget submarine crews at Kure Naval Base. All except the second and third from left, back row, died in the three attacks on Pearl Harbour, Sydney and Diego Suarez.

The Commandant Captain Sasaki sailed on I-22 and with him was First Sub-Lieutenant Matsuo acting as assistant to Commander Ageta and as a reserve member of the midget crew. Commandant Shojiro Tura, naval staff officer of the submarine fleet, travelled on I-18.

Loaded with their midgets the big submarines nosed through the Inland Sea and the Bungo Channel, headed for the Pacific by the shortest route on a course which would take them south of the Midway Islands. On the way training of the crews was intensified and work on the midgets was carried out on the decks to which they were clamped. Below decks, midget crews pored over charts of Hawaii and developed their attack plans.

On I-22, Matsuo worked with Lieutenant Iwasa over the plans of Pearl Harbour and briefed him with information gained from his recent visit there in the guise of an ordinary seaman. Meanwhile Commander Ageta, its captain, grappled with the problem of steering a submarine loaded with a midget. Although a midget weighed only forty-six tons, one-fiftieth the standard parent submarine's displacement of 2200 tons, the fact that it was loaded on the rear deck upset the big boat's original centre of gravity. Whenever I-22 set about submerging it was necessary to make adjustments to balance the extra weight on the rear deck.

Another danger was the weakness in the structure of a midget submarine. Any fracture of its hull caused by bad weather or enemy action, which allowed water to enter while it was clamped to the deck of its parent, would make it impossible for the larger boat to travel underwater. Because of this ever-present threat unusual precautions were needed in rough weather and even greater care had to be taken to avoid enemy action while in transit.

Air compression pipes and electrical charger cords ran along the upper deck of the carrier to the midget so that they were frequently put out of order by the motion of waves over the deck. Even when sailing on the surface the crew had to be ever watchful for damage.

The midget had been designed to withstand pressure while submerged to a depth of over 300 feet but, at that depth, her periscope and torpedo tubes were likely to leak and consequently the carrier submarine's freedom of movement under water was correspondingly restricted.

On one occasion, when I-22 and I-24 accidentally submerged to the midgets' maximum depth of 300 feet, the midgets' torpedoes were put out of action and the crew had to replace them from spares carried inside the parent submarines. This work had to be done on the surface and occupied a whole night.

Spaced at twenty-mile intervals the submarines cruised purposefully towards Hawaii for twenty days and arrived at a point about eight miles off Pearl Harbour on the evening of 6 December.

Four days earlier the main Japanese fleet had moved into a stand-by position about half-way to Hawaii and submarine crews had been told that the date fixed for the attack was 7 December.

Some 3500 miles east of Japan, no one in Pearl Harbour, port of the Hawaiian island of Oahu, had the slightest suspicion that five of the largest submarines afloat were steadily humping towards them something new in the way of warfare. Much less did they dream of the infinitely greater catastrophe in store for Pearl Harbour.

In spite of many warnings issued to naval and military commanders, Pearl Harbour's defences in early December 1941, were in a state of unbelievable unreadiness. The army's aircraft warning service was not operating; no regular reconnaissance or inshore patrols were maintained; and anti-aircraft batteries were neither manned nor supplied with ammunition. The anti-torpedo net closing the harbour was open!

Thus the stage was set for one of the most devastating surprise attacks in history.

Japan's naval strength at this time included ten aircraft carriers, eleven battleships, eighteen heavy and twenty-one light cruisers, 100 fleet destroyers and sixty-seven submarines.

Combined British, American and Dutch ships in the Pacific and Indian Oceans just before the Pearl Harbour attack consisted of four aircraft carriers, eleven battleships, fifteen heavy and thirty-two light cruisers, ninety-four destroyers and sixty submarines.

While Japanese envoys in Washington were still negotiating with the United States Secretary of State the Japanese war machine in the Pacific was poised, waiting for the button to be pressed.

Just after sunset on 6 December I-22 surfaced about eight miles south of Pearl Harbour Heads. From her conning tower Commander Ageta could see the neon lights of Oahu Island and a line of red lamps marking the airport. Across the water drifted the faint sounds of carefree jazz music.

Calling Lieutenant Iwasa and Sub-Lieutenant Matsuo to the conning tower, Commander Ageta ordered them to reconnoitre the harbour Heads. Matsuo pointed out the entrance to the harbour and explained the various channel markings, and then I-22 moved out to sea for final checking of the midget and to charge its secondary battery.

As I-22 moved shorewards again to launch her "baby", Matsuo made an impassioned plea to be allowed to accompany Iwasa. He had been excluded from training for the attack because of his absence on intelligence duty during final training stages.

"Why shouldn't I take part in this attack'!" he argued. "After all I know the area better than anyone here."

Captain Sasaki and Commander Ageta tried to dissuade him, but he sat resolutely in the briefing room until Lieutenant Iwasa spoke up.

"Do you want to kill me?" Iwasa demanded. "How can three men go on a two-man submarine? Even with two the air gets stuffy and hard to breathe. What do you think would happen with three of us in it?"

Matsuo was silenced by Iwasa's words and by the quiet dignity with which he spoke. Iwasa had been one of the chief planners of the attack and was the appointed leader of the mission.

"Don't be unreasonable," Iwasa argued. "The second and third attacks will probably be given in your charge." He held Matsuo's right hand and tapped him on the left shoulder. Tears came to Matsuo's eyes and he bent his head.

Before embarking on the midget, Lieutenant Iwasa and First Petty Officer Sasaki wiped their bodies clean with alcohol, sprayed perfume on their fresh underclothes and changed into new uniforms. Sasaki carried on his back his sabre wrapped in white cotton since the entrance to the midget was too narrow for him to carry it in his hand. After saying good-bye to the crew of I-22, Iwasa followed his friend into the midget and the hatch was locked.

From inside the midget Iwasa reported that everything was in readiness and the telephone cords were then cut.

Sometime before midnight I-22 submerged, the securing clamps were released and the midget started off for the harbour entrance. Similar preparations were going on in the other four carrier submarines and I-24's midget, after being held up until after midnight with a defective gyrocompass, finally set off with this important instrument out of action.

At daybreak on 7 December the periscope of a submarine was sighted off the entrance buoys to Pearl Harbour and the American destroyer *Ward* on patrol duty was alerted. Three hours later *Ward* located and sank a midget submarine. News of this action was immediately conveyed to the American command but, since a number of unconfirmed submarine sightings had been previously reported, little notice was taken of it.

At 7.45 a.m. another midget submarine was sighted inside the harbour net defences, but still the naval authorities issued no alert. Suddenly at 7.55 a.m. on 7 December (8 December in countries east of the International Dateline), swarms of Japanese planes roared in over Oahu and delivered the shattering king-hit which was to turn the Pacific into a vast battleground for the following three years.

Incredibly enough, the American aircraft warning station had detected the approach of a large flight of aircraft when it was some 130 miles away from Oahu nearly an hour before the attack, but no action was taken on the report made to the Central Information Centre.

The attacking Japanese aircraft broke into three formations, one of which concentrated on the naval aerodrome at Kaneoke Bay, another on the army air bases at Wheeler and Hickham Field, and the third on the warships in Pearl Harbour.

Japanese bombers made eight runs on the 86 ships of the American Pacific fleet anchored in the harbour and simultaneously one of the midget submarines which had successfully entered the harbour, fired a torpedo at the 11,000-ton seaplane tender *Curtis*. The midget missed her mark, however, and immediately invited depth charges from *Curtis* and her escorting destroyer which smashed in her bow. When the wrecked midget was subsequently salvaged one of the bodies recovered wore the uniform of a Lieutenant which, since the only full Lieutenant among the five crews was Iwasa, indicated that the victim had been from I-22's midget.

I-24's midget, in trouble with its gyro-compass, grounded on a shoal and there is no evidence that any of the other three achieved their purpose.

The air attack lasted less than two hours but by the time the planes were withdrawn the Japanese had achieved their aim of immobilising the American Pacific fleet.

Five battleships, three destroyers, a minelayer and a floating dock had been either sunk or seriously damaged and three battleships, three cruisers and a number of smaller craft were temporarily out of action. American casualties included 2117 naval and marine corps personnel dead as well as 226 army men.

When darkness fell on the night of 7 December the five carrier submarines surfaced and sailed to the rendezvous, seven miles southwest of Lanai, where they had arranged to pick up the returning midgets.

At this time the only communication received had been a radio message from Yokayama and Ueda in I-16's midget about twelve hours after the air attack: "We succeeded in the surprise." Two hours later the next and last message was picked up. "We cannot sail any more."

Assembled close enough for their commanders to see each other, the five submarines waited — but in vain. Several nights passed, but not one midget returned.

In the conning tower of I-22 the Captain, Commander Ageta, with Matsuo beside him, watched with bloodshot eyes night after night. Matsuo refused offers of relief by other officers and clung to the belief that at least one midget would return. Without their midgets, the carrier submarines turned their bows towards Japan.

Only three of the midgets were accounted for by the Americans.

Japanese sources record that the midget from I-24 had been delayed from the start by faults in its gyro-compass. It reached the harbour entrance but was attacked and depth charged by an American destroyer. After several more attempts to enter the bay it ran aground and stuck fast. Unable to fire their torpedoes and in danger of being overcome by foul gas, the crew emerged from their craft and were captured.

Whatever faith the Japanese higher command had in the ability of the 'midget to return safely with their crews it is clear that the midget submariners themselves were not so confident.

When officers commanding parent submarines were ordered to abandon hope of recovery and return to Kwajalein, their base in the Marshall Islands, they discovered that the midget men had all made very final personal arrangements before leaving on the Pearl Harbour mission. Each had written farewell messages to their parents and left directions for the disposal of personal effects.

3

Disheartened by the failure of any of the midgets to return after the attack, the five carrier submarine captains left Hawaii about 12 December. They headed for the Japanese base at Kwajalein in the Marshall Islands, I-22 pausing to shell Johnston Island on the way.

At the base Matsuo transferred to I-16 and returned to Japan to give his report on the midget submarines' performance. On arrival in Kure, he set to work studying information gathered by the other submarines' captains and looking for ways to remedy defects which had contributed to the tragic debacle at Pearl Harbour. Amidst the magnitude of the success of the air attack, the midgets' mission stood out as a stark failure.

At the same time Commander Shojiro Iura, staff officer of the 3rd Submarine Squadron who directed the midget operation at Pearl Harbour from I-18, was summoned to Tokyo to General Headquarters. There, Vice-Admiral Shigeru Fukutome, officer-in-charge of naval operations, addressed him: "Not one of the midgets has returned. In spite of that, the young officers are very keen to carry out the next plan. But only *once* more. If the midgets do not return next time I say there will be no more midget submarine operations."

Iura agreed that if the next operation, planned for Sydney and Diego Suarez in Madagascar, was not successful then further plans for the use of midget submarines should be dropped.

Work on improving the midgets to be used in the next attack was speeded up and the most important result was the invention of a connecting hatch through which the crew could enter from the parent submarine, even while submerged. In the bottom of the midget, which was to be secured to the top of the parent submarine, a circular hatch was constructed directly below the forward edge of the conning tower. Four securing lugs were spaced around the hatchway to provide grips for securing bolts. The hatch door, with a diameter of about seventeen inches, opened outwards on a hinge and was a quick release type controlled from inside the midget.

Two inches from the outer diameter of the hatchway was a circular collar, about two inches wide and one inch thick, which seated home in a corresponding circular groove on the hull of the parent submarine. The hatch door opened down into the parent submarine.

The gyro-compass was also improved and only two major faults remained unamended. One was the unsatisfactory operation of the helm in a horizontal direction and the other was lack of a suitable microphone which would enable the crew to detect the approach of enemy vessels.

By March 1942, Matsuo and other midget crew members were undergoing intensive training in the Seto Inland Sea for the next attack. Matsuo wrote to his family: "I may probably start for the front in the near future. So I wish to return home and see you and many other people at home. But as I am terribly busy I would be glad if you would come to see me at Kure. I shall be waiting for you. When you come, please worship for me at the Kikuchi Shrine and receive seven talismans of the shrine. It is my constant wish to go to a battle with the soul of the Kikuchi clan enshrined there.

"If possible I would ask you to give me the dagger from your treasure."

On 29 March Matsuo's father, Tsuruhiko, mother Matsue, sister Fujie and brother Jikyo went to see him at Kure. It was cherry blossom time and there were many cherry trees in colourful bloom around Kure Naval Headquarters.

Matsuo, whose face was pale and thin from hard training, met his family at the railway station and at the sight of him they thought he was ill. "Perhaps you are drinking too much?" his mother asked. Matsuo laughingly denied the suggestion but gave no explanation for his strained physical appearance.

That night the family had dinner together at a nearby hotel and Jikyo handed his brother the seven talismans of Kikuchi Jinya, an old shrine in Kyushu for the clan of Kikuchi Takemitsu. In 1336, when Japan was being ruled by two dynasties, three generations of the Kikuchis had fought for the southern dynasty. Three Kikuchis had become martyrs in 1348.

"Here's the dagger you've been longing for, Keiu," his father said, handing him the precious dagger in a purple sack made from the Obi (belt) worn by Keiu's mother on her wedding day. The dagger was named Kikuchi Senbonyari after the old story of a Kikuchi who was believed to have fastened the dagger to a long stick and used it to defeat a large number of his enemies.

"Thank you very much," Keiu said emotionally, staring at the icy blade. "I'll take it with me."

"The last time was Pearl Harbour," his father said. "This time too, I assume it will be in the far distance. It must be a difficult job, Keiu."

"Not so difficult, father," Keiu blushed and scratched his head.

"Anyway you must not waste your life. To value your life does not mean to live long — but to use it in the best way."

"What are you going to do with the seven talismans, Keiu?" his brother asked. "Aren't you a little greedy?"

"No," Keiu said. "I presented the talisman mother sent me last time to Lieutenant Iwasa when he went to the Pearl Harbour attack."

That night Keiu Matsuo and his brother got drunk together, and later Keiu spent a long time with his mother. The next morning he left his family without mentioning the coming attack on Sydney Harbour.

The month of April 1942 was one of great Japanese naval and air activity over vast areas, particularly to the north of Australia. In the Philippines the end was drawing near for the trapped Americans at Corregidor. In Burma Japanese forces were pushing the British and Indians back into India.

With Japanese bases established in New Britain, in the Solomons and on the north coast of New Guinea, Australia's island barrier had become an enemy springboard for further attacks on the continent itself.

Port Moresby had been warned that a crisis was imminent and on the mainland feverish defence preparations were in progress. Australian leaders believed that the Japanese aim was first to capture Port Moresby and then to advance south under cover of land-based aircraft. There was even talk of a defence line in the Brisbane area.

In the same month the Japanese navy finalised plans for submarine attacks on Sydney and Diego Suarez, which were to be carried out under the command of Vice-Admiral Chujun Daigo of the Sixth Fleet. This fleet consisted of four submarine squadrons, the 1st, 2nd, 3rd and 8th squadrons.

The 8th squadron was formed into a "Special Attack Group" consisting of ten I-class boats under the command of Rear-Admiral Noburo Ishizaki, a tough, fifty-two-year-old officer whose experience in underwater vessels was without peer in the Japanese navy.

Assigned the task of making simultaneous attacks on Diego Suarez in Madagascar and Sydney at the end of May 1942, Ishizaki divided his force into two groups, allotting five boats to each operation. The "Sydney Attack Group" under the command of Captain Hankyu Sasaki consisted of I-21 for aircraft reconnaissance and four midget submarine carriers I-22, I-24, I-27 and I-28.

Towards the end of April 1942 the Madagascar-bound force sailed to

Penang under the command of Rear-Admiral Ishizaki, who was flying his flag in the 2919-ton submarine I-I0, the largest boat of the force. Other boats in the Madagascar force were I-16, I-18, I-20 and I-30. Moving out into the Indian Ocean, they reconnoitred parts of the African coast and, as a result, the decision was made to send midgets into Diego Suarez Harbour on 31 May

At midnight on 30 May, I-16 and I-20 launched their midgets about ten miles from the harbour entrance and submerged to await their return. Both midgets entered the harbour successfully and discharged their torpedoes. One struck HMS *Ramillies*, causing some damage, but the ship was able to proceed to Durban with one compartment flooded. The other midget sank a large tanker.

After the attack the midget crews abandoned their craft and landed, being killed in subsequent fighting.

At the end of April, also, three boats of the Sydney-bound force, I-22, I-24 and I-28 were ordered to cover Japanese forces during the planned invasion of Port Moresby. I-22 had sailed back to the Honolulu area from Kwajalein at the end of December and then directed her course towards home, dropping anchor at Yokosuka Naval Port on 30 January 1942. From there she returned to Kure for renovations to enable her to embark the newly-modified midget.

With new fittings, but no midget, I-22 left Kure on 16 April and set a general course for Truk. On the way she pursued for a while the American Task Force which had carried out the first air raid on Tokyo. Reaching Truk on 28 April she then joined I-24 and I-28 for her part in the Battle of the Coral Sea. By 5 May the three submarines were in positions to attack shipping but no enemy targets came in sight.

Meanwhile, the other two submarines of the Sydney Attack Group, I-2I and I-27, proceeded down the east coast of Australia on reconnaissance. A sixth submarine, I-29, was also ordered to reconnoitre the Australian east coast with particular attention to the Sydney area.

On 2 May 1942 Australian coast watchers near Tulagi in the Solomon Islands reported the advance of Japanese ships. So by deduction, from this and other reports from Australian and American Intelligence, a definite invasion pattern emerged. Thus, for the first time in her history, Australia faced the dark threat of alien invasion.

Warned in advance, Rear-Admiral Fletcher of the American Navy brought his forces to a rendezvous south of the Solomons with other

American naval units under the command of Rear-Admiral Fitch. Fletcher's force included the aircraft carrier *Yorktown*, heavy cruisers *Astoria*, *Chester*, and *Portland*, six destroyers and the tanker *Neosho*. Under Fitch were the aircraft carrier *Lexington*, heavy cruisers *Minneapolis* and *New Orleans* and five destroyers. Fletcher took command of the combined forces while Fitch's ship began refuelling at sea from an oiler, guarded by the heavy cruiser *Chicago* and the destroyer *Perkins*.

On 2 May Admiral Fletcher learned that the Japanese were preparing to attack Port Moresby. He at once moved to the north-west, leaving Fitch to rendezvous with the Australian heavy and light cruisers *Australia* and *Hobart* under Rear-Admiral J. G. Crace. On 3 May Fletcher heard that the Japanese were landing at Tulagi so he launched three aircraft attacks from the *Yorktown* on shipping in Tulagi Harbour.

Two days later Fletcher rejoined Fitch and soon afterwards learned that a strong force of troop-carrying Japanese ships had left Rabaul, heading for Port Moresby under the protection of the aircraft carrier *Shoho*. This threatening spearhead appeared likely to approach Port Moresby through Jamard Passage in the Louisade Archipelago, while a separate Japanese force, centred around the carriers *Shokaku* and *Zuikaku*, was moving into the Coral Sea round San Cristobel in the southern Solomons.

On the morning of 7 May aircraft from the *Lexington* and *Yorktown* located the Japanese carrier *Shoho*, which they bombed and finally torpedoed. The *Shoho* sank within a few minutes and the troop transports were ordered to turn back to Rabaul. About the same time Japanese aircraft from the *Shokaku* and *Zuikaku* sank the tanker *Neosho* mistaking it for an aircraft carrier.

On the following morning the main battle began off the Louisades but not a single shot was exchanged between opposing ships. Instead, the aircraft carriers manoeuvred to launch their planes and avoid attack. At the same time land-based Japanese planes from Rabaul and Australian planes based in the Cairns-Townsville-Cloncurry area took off to join the battle.

Apart from the *Shoho* the Japanese lost no ships although some were badly damaged. On the other hand, the Americans lost the carrier *Lexington* and the destroyer *Sims*. The importance of the battle for Australia was that the attack on Port Moresby was staved off and air attacks planned on the Australian north-east coast by the carriers Shokaku and Zuikaku did not eventuate.

In spite of the Coral Sea setback to their plans for invading Port Moresby, the Japanese decided to go ahead with the midget submarine attack on Sydney. Accordingly, on 11 May, I-22, I-24, I-27 and I-28 were ordered to make for Truk, the Japanese naval base in the Carolines, to embark the waiting midget submarines and their crews.

On the morning of 17 May I-28 was sighted, not far from Truk, by the American submarine *Tautog* bound for Fremantle. Caught on the surface, with numerals and men on the bridge plainly visible, I-28 was hit by a torpedo from *Tautog*. The damaged Japanese submarine tried to fight back with her deck gun until a second torpedo striking home under her conning tower brought her career to a bitter end. The remaining three submarines reached Truk safely.

On a hot afternoon on May 15, I-22 embarked her midget from the *Chiyoda*. The midget's crew, Keiu Matsuo, now a Lieutenant, and Petty Officer Tsuzuku came aboard. The two men saluted I-22's crew with whom they had previously worked on the Pearl Harbour attack.

Matsuo had changed a lot during the five months since he had been away from I-22, but Commander Ageta was well pleased and happy that Matsuo appeared to be on very good terms with his mate Tsuzuku. The midget itself incorporated many of the recently devised improvements, including the connecting hatch which enabled passage from the carrier to the midget under water. It was now also possible for the midget's secondary batteries to be charged from the carrier submarine and for air to be sent through a newly-devised pipe.

Before the Pearl Harbour attack the midget submarine operation had been a jealously guarded secret even from the carrier submarines' torpedo group and engineers. Before leaving Truk for Sydney the secret was disclosed and this resulted in improved understanding and more energetic co-operation between crews.

On 20 May 1942, I-22, I-24 and I-27 sailed for Australian waters with midgets clamped on their hulls. I-22's midget crew consisted of Lieutenant Keiu Matsuo and Petty Officer Masao Tsuzuku; I-24's crew were Sub-Lieutenant Katsuhisa Ban and Petty Officer Mamori Ashibe; and I-27's crew, Lieutenant Kenshi Chuma and Petty Officer Takeshi Ohmori.

While the three midget carriers were preparing for the assault on Sydney Harbour, the other two sea-going submarines of the force, I-2I and I-29, had been busy on reconnaissance. Both carried float planes and while I-21 patrolled in the Suva area, I-29 made her presence felt close to the Australian coast. On 16 May I-29 shelled the Russian steamer *Wellen* within thirty miles of Newcastle. Hunted by HMAS *Arunta* and the American destroyer *Perkins*, she lay submerged in the area and eluded detection by only surfacing at night to recharge her batteries.

On 23 May while I-22, I-24 and I-27 were en route from Truk, and I-21 was approaching Australian waters from Fijian seas, I-25 sent up her seaplane to reconnoitre over Sydney. The plane returned undetected after flying over the harbour to report the presence of "battleships and cruisers".

About 27 May 1942, the Sydney Attack Group assembled off the New South Wales coast — about thirty-five miles north-east of Sydney. Ashore, naval authorities in Sydney had no inkling of the presence of five large enemy submarines so close to home. On 29 May, however, a report from New Zealand suggested that enemy naval units could be very close to Sydney. On the same day the National Emergency Service issued two standby warnings in Sydney and Newcastle — one at 5.31 a.m. and another at 4.28 p.m. Unidentified aircraft had been sighted. However, they turned out to be friendly.

In the early hours of the following morning I-21 launched her float plane from a position thirty-five miles north-east of Sydney Heads. The pilot Susumo Ito, a former fishing tackle salesman, took off from a choppy sea and, accompanied by an observer, headed for Sydney.

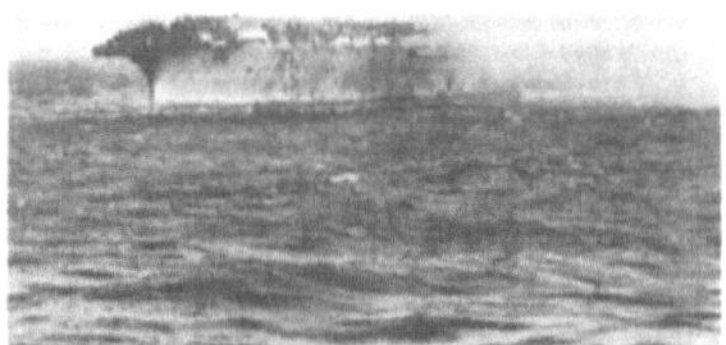

Top: United States aircraft carrier *Lexington* burning following Coral Sea battle, 8 May 1942.

Bottom: Japanese submarine I-5, similar to the mother submarines which carried the midgets to Sydney.

Burning normal navigation lights, he was over the harbour by 4 a.m. Ito flew along the path of the Manly ferry as low as 600 feet, thus enabling his observer to make sketches of the opening in Sydney's submarine boom as well as naval units anchored around Garden Island. The observer made notes on "battleships, cruisers and other units". What he saw, in fact, were thirteen warships including the American cruiser *Chicago*, the destroyer *Perkins* and the destroyer tender *Dobbin*; the Royal Netherlands submarine *K9*; the cruiser HMAS *Canberra* and the auxiliary cruiser *Westralia*.

The plane was seen and heard by people on Garden Island who made enquiries without obtaining any results. Other reports of unidentified aircraft, subsequent to those from Garden Island, caused air raid warnings to be issued in the Sydney-Newcastle area. Although fighter aircraft carried out a search nothing unusual was discovered.

Circling the *Chicago* twice, Ito observed the flash of oxy welding torches at nearby Cockatoo Island. He flew on over the Harbour Bridge and then headed out to sea to rejoin I-21. He found it waiting on the surface but, over-eager to impart the exciting information he had gathered, he capsized the plane when alighting on the steadily rising sea.

The plane sank and Ito and his observer had to swim through icy water to reach the submarine.

When the airmen had made their report, Captain Sasaki decided to launch the attack as soon as darkness fell over Sydney. The target date was 31 May.

4

To prevent such a raid as Sasaki planned there were fixed anti-submarine defences, in the shape of indicator loops, at Sydney Heads which warned of any vessel crossing. Two of the six outer indicator loops, however, were out of action but both of the inner loops, one in fifteen fathoms and the other in seven fathoms, were in operation.

An anti-torpedo boom at the inner entrance to the harbour had almost been completed, leaving gaps of 960 feet at the western end and 900 feet at the eastern end. Unnetted piles were in position in the western gap and the boom defence was lit by searchlight. An anti-submarine vessel HMAS Yandra was on duty in the loops area, a channel patrol boat HMAS *Yarroma* was on station at West Gate and four naval auxiliary patrol boats were cruising in the harbour.

Behind this security screen shipping conditions in the harbour were normal. No large transports were in port but, in addition to warships mentioned before were HMAS vessels *Adelaide*, *Bungaree*, *Kanimbla*, *Whyalla*, *Geelong*, *Kuttabul*, which was anchored off Garden Island, and an Indian ship HMIS *Bombay*.

On the night of 31 May, Sydney's weather was wintry, with the sky dark and overcast. Whenever the clouds parted, however, a full moon illuminated the harbour. Outside the Heads, the sea was broken and uneasy.

During the afternoon of 31 May a number of ships, including the hospital ship *Oranje*, had entered the harbour, but Sasaki had let them pass unmolested. He was after bigger fish and believed that the battleship *Warspite* was among the targets waiting in the harbour.

About 5 p.m. the three carrier submarines I-22, I-24 and I-27 released their midgets seven miles off the heads and in rapidly waning light the attacking crews took bearing from the dark bulk of land etched against the western horizon. At periscope depth the three midgets moved towards their goal.

Lieutenant Jokai Chuma in I-27's midget was first to reach the Heads and at 8 p.m. crossed the indicator loop undetected by following close behind ferries and other traffic. A few minutes later, however, the midget's propeller became entangled in the torpedo net near the West Gate and she became hopelessly trapped like a fly in a spider web.

It was then, at about 8.15 p.m., that Maritime Services Board watchman

James Cargill noticed suspicious movement through one of the gaps in the submarine boom. After rowing across to investigate and seeing what appeared to be two oxygen bottles floating in the harbour, he reported his discovery to Lieutenant H. C. Eyers in command of the naval patrol boat HMAS *Yarroma*, and then rowed back with a sailor to take another look.

This time there was no doubt that the "oxygen bottles" were torpedo tube caps and *Yarroma*, after identifying the object as a small submarine, prepared to open fire.

Meanwhile, Lieutenant Katsuhisa Ban in I-24's midget had crossed the indicator loop at 9.48 p.m., evading the net, and undetected entered the harbour waters. At periscope depth he stealthily moved towards the man-o'-war anchorage, bent on torpedoing *Chicago*. I-27's midget struggled to escape from the net but in vain. Suddenly at 10.35 p.m., as *Yarroma* prepared to fire, a loud explosion in the net signalled the firing of self-demolition charges which reduced the intruder to a mass of twisted metal and demolished crew.

The roar of the explosion hurled debris forty feet into the air and heralded the beginning of the wildest night of harbour violence in Sydney's history. It also brought Captain Bode, *Chicago's* commanding officer, in haste from the shore to his ship.

Seventeen minutes after the first explosion in the net, *Chicago's* gun crews sighted a submarine some 200 yards off the ferry wharf at Garden Island and immediately opened fire with four inch guns and Oerlikons. HMAS *Whyalla*, nearby, also sighted the midget and opened fire with machine guns.

Pinpointed by searchlights and pelted with pom-pom and red tracer bursts, Lieutenant Ban steered I-24's midget away towards the Harbour Bridge, passing close to Garden Island and almost colliding with the motor boat *Nestor* as he hastened to evade the deadly fire.

Making good his escape Lieutenant Ban turned towards the north shore and manoeuvred to take up a firing position aimed at *Chicago* which, from that point, stood out in silhouette against the floodlit dockyard.

By this time alerted patrol boats were roaring up and down the harbour and probing searchlights raked the surface of the water.

About the same time as the *Chicago* opened fire on I-24's midget, Lieutenant Matsuo was navigating I-22's midget between the outer and inner indicator loops, on the ocean side of the anti-torpedo boom. HMAS *Lauriana* patrolling in the area sighted a turbulence in the water and, switching on her searchlights, clearly illuminated the midget's conning tower less than eighty feet away.

Unarmed herself, *Lauriana* signalled HMAS *Yandra* and she too observed the midget some 400 yards from Hornby Light. She prepared to ram, but Matsuo evaded this action and reappeared one hundred yards astern of *Yandra*, turning slowly to starboard. For five minutes *Yandra* lost sight of the midget, then again sighted her conning tower 500 yards off. Racing over, *Yandra* dropped six depth-charges which damaged but did not disable the I-22's midget. Matsuo crash-dived to the bottom to wait.

Bursting depth-charges and gunfire roused the residents of harbour-side suburbs and hundreds of them, believing an air raid was in progress, rose and hurriedly dressed. Some thought an earthquake had occurred, while others merely turned in their beds and attributed the noise to harmless blasting.

For residents with a harbour view the picture was dramatic. Across the moonlit water searchlights converged to one point like the spokes of a wheel. Harbour patrol boats scurried back and forth like mosquitoes, port and starboard lights winking. Through the rays of the searchlights heavy smoke hung like a fog and muffled explosions intermingled with the rattle of heavy machine guns.

The Sydney Morning Herald of 2 June 1942, records the experiences of passengers on two ferryboats, who had a grandstand view of the grim hunt for the midget submarine:

"Passengers on a ferryboat which left Circular Quay saw most of the attack on the submarines. There were 27 passengers on the ferryboat as guns began to blaze, some only a few yards away.

"At first it was thought that naval practice with blank shells was being carried out but a defence order was sent to the captain to go hard-astern.

"Passengers said that by this time guns were blazing and searchlights were flooding the harbour, which also was brightly lit by a full moon. In the moonlight some passengers said they saw what they took to be the grey periscope of a submarine, but it disappeared so quickly that they did not have time to positively identify it.

"Tracer bullets, which threw a red light, were fired across the harbour. A shell of large calibre threw a spout of water hundreds of feet in the air

"Passengers on another ferryboat, numbering about forty, had the experience of seeing large calibre guns blazing, seemingly directly at them.

"The muzzles of the guns, however, had been canted so that high explosive shells would strike the water at least a mile from the ferry and, as each shell struck, water was hurled skywards and the night resounded to the violent explosions of the shells."

At thirty minutes after midnight, Lieutenant Ban aimed I-24's midget at the *Chicago* as she was about to slip from the buoy and fired two torpedoes from the direction of Bradley's Head.

One torpedo missed its target and ran ashore on rocks covered with a heap of rope near the gun wharf on the east side of Garden Island. It failed to explode. The other passed under the Netherlands submarine *K9* and hit the harbour bottom under HMAS *Kuttabul*, a former Sydney passenger ferry on commission as a depot ship. This torpedo exploded and sank the *Kuttabul*— killing nineteen ratings and wounding ten.

The Sydney Sun of 2 June 1942, records an interview with Mr M. N. Cumming who had walked on board the *Kuttabul* no more than four minutes before the torpedo struck:

"I heard a crash and found myself hurled through a glass door and then a window…I was lucky to escape with only a few scratches from the broken glass."

He found that men in a section of the ferry near him were trapped so he called to another man to come to his assistance.

He never found out the name of the man whom he called but gave him high praise for the way in which he set about the rescues.

"We saw the water rising and we just stripped off all our clothes and dived to the rescue. We saw a man's arm sticking out of the water.

"All the time the water was coming higher into the ferry cabin as she was settling down.

Top and bottom: HMAS *Kuttabul* after being sunk by a torpedo fired by I-24's midget.

"We grabbed the arm and pulled and brought our man to the surface. He was alive and only the prompt action of my fellow-rescuer saved him.

"Quickly we helped him ashore."

Cumming said that his first impression was that a bomb had been dropped. After the crash of the first explosion he thought he heard a second, but it probably was only the timbers of the old ferry shattering into splintered fragments.

He said it felt eerie to walk along the torn, ripped deck of the ferry.

One moment he would be on an even planking and next he would drop through a gaping hole and find himself up to his neck in water.

An eye witness who saw the ferry hit said that the whole ferry lifted as though she were on the top of an enormous wave, then settled down again, sinking at the stern. Pieces of wood flew into the air and half of the steering wheel was blown away. The whole of the after part of the ferry was wrecked and within a few minutes it had submerged with only the upper deck remaining above water.

One man killed was a survivor from the battleship HMS *Repulse*, sunk off Malaya the previous December. Another had escaped from the bombed HMS *Cornwall*.

Seaman William Williams of Inverell complained that he had been in danger spots in England, the Mediterranean, Indian and Pacific Oceans for two years without receiving a scratch yet had to receive serious injury in his home port of Sydney.

Many of the men on *Kuttabul* had been on deck earlier watching the "fireworks" when the first alarm had been raised. When the commotion had died down they returned to their bunks and were asleep when the torpedo struck.

I-24's midget, having discharged her torpedoes, was now harmless, but Lieutenant Matsuo in I-22's midget was still at large waiting for an opportunity to fire his tin fishes. While the hunt continued Matsuo played possum at the harbour entrance for nearly three hours until at 3 a.m., his midget was sighted by the outbound *Chicago*, less than a cable's length away.

Two minutes later I-22's midget crossed the indicator loop and slipped unperceived into the harbour. Alerted by the *Chicago* that another midget was still at large the hunt was intensified, particularly by the patrol boats *Sea Mist, Steady Hour* and *Yarroma* in the West Gate area.

After two hours' fruitless search the minesweeper *Goonambee* on patrol from Bradley Head to the West Gate, sighted a suspicious object in Taylor's Bay. She signalled the *Sea Mist* for assistance and, rushing to help, *Sea Mist* discovered I-22's midget on the surface in the act of submerging.

Sea Mist dropped two depth-charges and fired her Very lights. The roar of exploding cannisters brought *Yarroma* and *Steady Hour* to the scene, the attack was renewed and maintained until after dawn.

At length, rising oil and great belching bubbles of air told of destruction wrought on the midget below and final confirmation of its destruction came when *Steady Hour's* anchor fouled the submarine's hull.

Attempts to salvage I-22's midget from the bed of Taylor's Bay began later in the day and divers who went down to investigate were amazed to find the submarine's engines still running.

The midget's torpedo tubes still contained their torpedoes and her nose protection gear indicated that she had struck a submerged object in the Harbour. The damage had jammed her torpedo caps, which prevented her from firing. In addition, there was evidence of considerable damage caused by depth-charges and the after section of the midget had completely broken off at a joint.

Examining the wreckage, divers discovered that a live torpedo had been partly released from one tube and that another was intact in a second tube.

Naval submarine salvage experts decided that the job of raising the midget would be highly dangerous and that the only lift possible without exploding the torpedoes would have to be by the bow.

After hammering the midget's nose-protection gear into a position to form a cage which would hold the torpedoes from slipping out, the divers began knocking a ridge around the midget's hull to enable the wire hawsers to grip.

There was no response to their knocking from inside the hull so the divers concluded that anyone inside would have been drowned by water which poured in through fractured seams in the plating.

At 5 p.m. the midget's engine was still running as the divers continued with the delicate task of hammering grip ridges for the hawsers.

By Tuesday morning, 2 June, the engine had stopped running and work continued until next day when the first attempt to lift I-22's midget was made with a fifty-ton crane. The hawser, however, parted below the water under a forty-ton strain.

Next day another attempt was made and the bow was lifted until about fifteen feet of it was visible, with the stern resting on the bottom. Before attempting the final lift, however, the salvage party decided to tow the midget to shallow water. Accordingly a tug put a line on the floating crane *Samson*, which held the wreck, and the difficult tow started.

Anxiously watched by red and blue-bereted divers in thick woollen sweaters, the big crane began slowly moving the warped midget submarine into shallow water in Taylor's Bay and, after three hours, came to a stop.

By this time word that the submarine was coming up had spread around the waterfront and at 2 p.m. large crowds were lining the foreshores of the Bay. In small boats just off shore American and Australian newsmen, who had been following the drama for days, stood by as the crane's big hook descended into the water.

The furnace of the crane, stoked with piles of wood, suddenly gushed out clouds of smoke and steam and the wire hawser snapped taut.

The Sydney Daily Telegraph of 5 June described the dramatic moment as the wrecked hull broke the surface of the water:

"There was a tense silence. No one on the crane spoke. Then suddenly at 3.30 p.m. the cutting gear on the bow of the submarine broke surface.

"Naval ratings took off their hats out of respect to seamen believed to be inside the hull.

"Just beneath the cutting gear, the war-head of a torpedo jutted out, the cap of the tube caught in the cutting gear. Oil smeared the surface of the harbour as the stem rose slowly six feet out of the water.

"The submarine was then tilted at an angle of about 45 degrees. It was held there momentarily until another line was put around the hull to straighten the submarine, and point the live torpedo skyward to prevent escape."

Damage to the midget's nose-protection gear suggested that she had struck a submerged object in the harbour and that the jolt from this collision had jammed her torpedo tubes, preventing them from firing. The deadly effects of depth charging were also very evident, the after section having been completely broken off at a joint some distance from the stern.

Top and bottom: Salvage operations on the shattered hulk of one of the Japanese midget submarines.

Inside, the bodies of Lieutenant Keiu Matsuo and Petty Officer Masao Tsuzuku were found, each shot through the head. Their untouched rations of dried fish, biscuits, plums, chocolate and caramels were a grim witness to their sudden ending. The men had apparently killed themselves, although it is possible that Tsuzuku may have attempted to escape since his boots had been removed.

A ceremonial sword bearing the name of Lieutenant Matsuo was found hanging in the control room.

On 5 June the stern half of I-27's midget containing the bodies of Lieutenant Chuma and Petty Officer Ohmori was disentangled from the submarine net defences and brought to the surface.

The job of recovery was simple compared with raising the first midget as there was no danger from undischarged torpedoes. These were found intact in the forward section which at the time was in too shattered a condition to be raised.

Salvage operations began at dawn and by mid-day the wreck had been raised on an even keel from about forty-six feet of water. When the midget broke the surface the hatch of its conning tower was open and a tangled mass of wire was wound around the propeller shaft and guard.

A twelve foot strip of the forepart of the hull wrapped around the conning tower like so much tissue paper was evidence of the tremendous force of the explosion which had ripped it open.

The remains of the midget were raised by a huge crane fixed to a steam driven punt and then carried for more than two miles where they were landed ashore alongside I-22's midget.

I-24's midget, with First Sub-Lieutenant Ban and First Petty Officer Ashibe aboard, had been the only one to fire her torpedoes. After evading the patrols she re-crossed the boom defences and escaped from the harbour at about 2 a.m. on 1 June. What happened to her after that is not known but it is presumed that she finally sank as a result of damage inflicted earlier by *Chicago's* guns.

Top: Salvage operations on one of the Japanese midget submarines.

Bottom: Close-up of the special harbour defence net cutter fixed on the bow of each midget submarine.

The first official announcement on the raid was a special communique issued on 1 June by General Headquarters in Melbourne which read:

"In an attempted raid on Sydney three enemy midget submarines are believed to have been destroyed, one by gunfire, two by depth-charges.

"The enemy's attack was completely unsuccessful. Damage was confined to one small harbour vessel of no military value."

Details of the nineteen naval ratings killed and ten wounded in the sinking of the *Kuttabul* were released over the following few days and on 3 June the burial of eight Australian victims took place at Rookwood Cemetery. They were accorded full naval honours and a firing party drawn from Navy personnel fired a volley over their graves.

Proud of their own fighting men, Australians felt duty bound to recognise the quality of courage even when displayed by their enemies.

Accordingly, when the bodies of four Japanese crew members of the sunken midgets were recovered, it was decided, without hesitation, that they be given the honourable burial which Australia would expect her own gallant dead to be given in similar circumstances.

Since cremation is the usual Japanese method of disposing of the dead, the remains of Lieutenant Keiu Matsuo, Lieutenant Kenshi Chuma, Petty Officer Masao Tsuzuku and Petty Officer Takeshi Ohmori were cremated with full naval honours at Rookwood Cemetery, Sydney, on 9 June 1942. The funeral, attended by the Rear-Admiral-in-charge, Sydney, was carried out with complete ceremony. The coffins were covered with a Japanese flag and a volley was fired by a Naval saluting party.

The ceremony was similar to that carried out for the burial of Australian naval victims of the attack and the ashes of the dead Japanese were placed in the columbarium at Eastern Suburbs Crematorium for return to Japan later when opportune.

The raid had proved a dismal failure. Even its subsidiary purpose of causing dismay and alarm on the Australian mainland was not achieved. On the contrary, the vigilance of Australian naval units in frustrating the attack became a cause for jubilation and in Sydney it served to inspire stronger determination to prevent the repetition of similar attacks.

From London, on 6 June, came an echo of the midget submarine attack on Diego Suarez Harbour in Madagascar, which had been carried out simultaneously with the raid on Sydney.

Top: Naval firing party firing a volley over the graves of men of HMAS *Kuttabul* killed in the midget submarine raid.

Bottom: Funeral of the crew of the Japanese midget submarines.

The British Admiralty denied a Japanese claim to have damaged a British battleship and a light cruiser in Diego Suarez Harbour and went on to say that it had no intention of giving the enemy any details which could assist them in future operations.

At the same time news from another source in London, reporting that two disguised Japanese naval officers had been shot near Diego Suarez while trying to escape, indicated that the Madagascar midget submarine raid had been as big a failure as the Sydney debacle.

It was learned afterwards that two submarines, I-16 and I-20, had launched midgets at midnight on 30 May at a point ten miles from the entrance to Diego Suarez Harbour. Neither of the midgets returned, but their crews had landed and been killed in subsequent fighting.

5

The years of jealously guarded secrecy surrounding the construction and operation of midget submarines had gone for nothing when the Americans captured one intact during the raid on Pearl Harbour. It was seventy-five feet long, five and a half feet wide, had a conning tower four and a half feet high and a maximum speed of twenty-four knots. Crewed by two men it carried two eighteen-inch torpedoes and some 300 pounds of high explosive for use as demolition charges against ships or for self-destruction to prevent the midget from falling into enemy hands.

At the time of its capture in Pearl Harbour, American naval experts calculated that it had been launched from a ship about 100 miles from Hawaii. They believed that the Japanese were carrying midgets in the holds of converted freighters, probably disguised as Allied merchantmen, and that they lowered them into the water by cranes when the mother ship came within striking distance of an objective.

After the Sydney Harbour attack the Australian Navy lost no time in ferreting out any secrets contained in the wrecked hulls on the harbour bed. Salvage operations had started immediately after the action ended and from the two boats recovered it was found possible to reconstruct one complete midget. This was done fairly easily since fittings in both submarines were identical.

Examination disclosed the following specifications of the captured midgets.

Overall length: 80.5 feet.
Forward section: 17 feet.
Midship section: 34 feet 11 inches.
After section: 22 feet 4 inches.
Noseguard: 3 feet.
Diameter amidships: 6 feet.
Height of conning tower: 4 feet 6 inches, with additional guard structure 15 inches high.

Of greater interest to the Australian Navy was evidence of the method by which the midget was attached to the top of the hull of a parent submarine and the ingenious interconnecting hatch through which crew members could transfer from parent to midget while submerged.

Other features of the midget included a saw-tooth net-cutter, a steel framework structure to protect the nose and a guard cage built around the contra-revolving four-bladed propellers.

For its size the midget was well-equipped. Its periscope was capable of extending seven or eight feet above the top of the conning tower, giving it a maximum periscope depth of seventeen and a half feet and other important installations included a gyro-compass, magnetic compass, wireless transmitter, underwater sound listening apparatus and telephone communication for use when midget and parent were linked.

Rations discovered in the wrecked midgets included soda biscuits, dried fish, pickled plums, peas, chocolate, caramels, mineral water, wine and whisky.

Each midget carried two eighteen-inch torpedoes and the unexploded torpedo recovered at Garden Island had a warhead five feet eight inches long and seventeen and a half inches in diameter. In each midget self-demolition charges had been fitted both forward and aft.

From documents found in both recovered midgets and by reconstructing events which took place during the attack, the Australian Navy was also able to obtain an accurate picture of the operational planning behind the use of midget submarines.

In the wrecked hull of I-27's midget, call sign lists were found together with operational orders. Operational abbreviations for use when in range of the enemy, for use by aircraft and by midget submarines were also discovered.

On photostat copies of Admiralty charts, large photographs of targets had been placed and these included pictures of Garden Island, Hawkesbury River Railway Bridge, Broken Hill Proprietary Limited steel works, the floating dock at Newcastle, Cockatoo Island and Walsh Island shipyards. There was also a large sheet of photographs of various areas and targets including infra-red aerial photographs of Sydney Harbour taken from Australian periodicals published in 1938. I-22's midget contained lists of call signs allocated to float planes attached to I-21 and I-29 and charts on which a course to Garden Island had been plotted in pencil.

Lieutenant Matsuo's plans had been disrupted however when he was first depth-charged by *Sea Mist* in Taylor's Bay at 5 a.m. He had obviously attempted to launch an attack as both torpedo tubes of his midget had been fired but the torpedoes had jammed and failed to operate.

Above: From the remains of I-22 and I-27's midgets one composite midget submarine was reconstructed.

This suggests that he had tried to fire in a hurry and was prompted by, or interrupted by, *Sea Mist's* initial attack. He probably dived to the bottom where the torpedo bow caps received the damage which prevented later release.

Three more hours of intermittent depth-charging by *Yarroma* and *Steady Hour* had inflicted the great damage later evident when the midget was finally recovered.

Midgets used in the Sydney attack were five feet longer than those used at Pearl Harbour and had wider beams and thicker plating. They also had more efficient net cutting gear and greater periscope height. Australian naval authorities concluded from their examination that the midgets were not intended as suicide craft, as was the popular belief of most Australians. They estimated that a midget could operate for a period of up to a week provided it could surface at night so that the crew could exercise and fresh ventilation be obtained.

The idea of a suicide submarine or human torpedo nevertheless was being considered separately by the Japanese at this time, but the need for such desperate measures was still far off.

The Japanese Navy did not accept the idea of sending its men to certain death until the end of 1944 when it formed its "Kaiten" units. The "Kaiten", meaning "the turn toward heaven", was a small submarine fitted with a tiny compartment in which the pilot rode on a one-way mission. It was the undersea counterpart of the Kamikaze and was used with reasonable success in the final naval battles of World War II. Its effectiveness lay in the fact that the pilot steered it to the target with the aid of a periscope. Once launched he could not survive in any event.

Several Kaiten units were formed and the suicide craft, with their crews, were carried by parent submarines and launched against ships under way in the ocean as well as against anchored targets.

Mochitsura Hashimoto, the torpedo officer on I-24 during the midget submarine attack on Pearl Harbour had, towards the end of the war, become a submarine captain in command of the Kaiten carrier I-58. In his book *Sunk*, he describes the fanatical lengths to which the Japanese submarine service was driven after the Americans had recaptured Guam and begun moving on Okinawa.

Young, highly-trained naval men were calmly loaded into their torpedoes and fired at enemy destroyers or aircraft carriers as though they were expendable fuses. The willingness with which these patriotic youths went to certain death and the pre-ordained futility of all their efforts makes pathetic reading on the terribleness of war.

In their use of midget submarines, and to an ultimate degree with the Kaitens, the Japanese Navy's attitude to the lives of their own people contrasts vividly with similar underwater techniques employed by the British, Germans, Italians and Australians. These nations spared no expense or effort to ensure the survival of their crews no matter how high the stakes.

An Australian .enterprise, which had objectives similar to those set by the Japanese for their midget submarine crews in the Sydney Harbour attack, was a mission known as Operation Jaywick — directed against Singapore Harbour in the spring of 1943.

This sneak attack project was launched from Australia by fourteen men, under the command of Major Ivan Lyon of the Gordon Highlanders, and involved the use of two-men canoes carrying limpet mines.

The flimsy canoes and their crews were transported to an island near Singapore in a former Japanese fishing vessel, the *Kofuku Maru*, which had been saved during the fall of Singapore and sailed to Bombay. Brought to Sydney by cargo ship it was renamed the *Krait* and made ready for one of the most daring voyages of World War II.

The aim of Operation Jaywick was identical with the purpose of the Japanese midget submarine raid on Sydney, namely to surprise and sink enemy shipping in its home harbour and upset enemy morale with the hidden fear of a surprise attack.

The Australian operation depended for its success on daring and deceit. The attacking canoe men, after leaving Exmouth Gulf in Western Australia, sailed in the *Krait* through Lombok Strait and across the Japanese-controlled South China Seas to the Rhio Archipelago and Singapore.

The *Krait* (seventy-eight feet long and ten feet six inches wide) brazenly travelled 2000 miles through enemy territory in twenty-one days and, on 27th September 1943, three two-men canoes loaded with explosives, were stealthily paddled into Singapore Harbour.

Ronald McKie in his book, *The Heroes*, gives a moving account of the mission leader, Major Lyon, and Able Seaman Huston paddling their tiny canoe through Japanese shipping lying at anchor in the harbour, to fix a load of deadly explosives against the plates of a loaded enemy oil tanker. In pitch darkness they performed the delicate task within feet of unsuspecting Japanese sailors and then paddled out of the harbour to rejoin the waiting *Krait*.

In contrast with the tragic results of the midget raid on Sydney, all men who took part in Operation Jaywick returned safely to Exmouth Gulf on 19 October 1943. They had sunk the *Hakusan Maru*, of 2197 tons, and the *Kizan Maru*, of 5077 tons.

An attempt to repeat this raid the following year met with disastrous results. The 1944 raid, led also by Major Ivan Lyon, was a submarine-carried operation in which electrically-powered submersible metal boats were to be used to attach limpet mines to shipping in Singapore Harbour.

The submersible boats, nicknamed *Sleeping Beauties*, were twelve feet long and similar in shape to Eskimo kayaks. Each held one man who sat inside in front of a half steering wheel and control panel. Each operator, who was equipped with oxygen mask and container — an outfit similar to that of a frogman —controlled his craft in a porpoise fashion as he approached his target. Surfacing near his objective, with his eyes just above water level, the operator would submerge and reappear again alongside his target. He would then affix his limpets, submerge and escape.

Operation Rimau, employing these techniques, involved twenty-two men under Major Lyon and Lieutenant Page who were taken to a point near Singapore in the submarine HMS *Porpoise*. There, they captured a Malay junk to use as a mother ship for their fifteen *Sleeping Beauties* and proceeded on towards their objective. *Porpoise* meanwhile returned to Fremantle with the captured Malay junk crew.

An unforeseen encounter with a patrol boat, however, put an end to hopes for this daring scheme. In the resulting skirmishes twelve of the twenty-two men were killed fighting or died trying to escape.

Top: The *Krait*. This former Japanese fishing boat was used to transport the members of Operation Jaywick into enemy territory to raid Singapore Harbour in the spring of 1943.

Bottom: Officers and men of Operation Jaywick. In the middle of the front row is Major Ivan Lyon, leader of the mission.

The remaining ten were captured and given the treatment usually reserved for Japanese heroes. Since they were enemies the treatment also included honourable execution by beheading. This was carried out in Singapore on 7 July 1945. Among the bravest to die in this fashion was Lieutenant R.C. Page, a hero of the successful raid the previous year.

A curious aspect of the court-martial of the Rimau Operation survivors was the praise lavished on them for their spirit and determination by the prosecuting officer, Major Kimiya, a graduate in law from Tohuku Imperial University and a former civilian lawyer. He compared the prisoners' deeds with those of various heroes in Japanese history and expressed the belief that anything short of death would be unworthy of them. The last moments of heroes, he maintained, had to be historic and dramatic.

In asking for the death sentence the prosecutor referred to the Japanese midget submarine crews who died in the Sydney Harbour attack and to the respect shown the dead by the Australian Government in having them buried with full military honours.

Thus an act of humanity which Australians had performed as a matter of normal civilised behaviour profoundly affected the Japanese. News of this chivalry must have been widespread among the various services.

Not long after the midget attack in May 1942, Australian prisoners of war working on the docks in Singapore were told about it by their Japanese guards and, for a brief while, the guards' treatment reflected their appreciation of what they regarded as Australia's chivalry.

Some three weeks after the execution of the Rimau men two British midget submarines also penetrated Johore Strait and, on 31 July 1945, one of them damaged the already partly disabled heavy cruiser *Takao*.

The British midgets were much more sophisticated craft than those used by the Japanese in Sydney Harbour. Manned by a crew of four men the British X-type midget was constructed so as to permit a frogman to emerge from it underwater, place explosive charges against enemy ships, and then re-enter by the same way as he had gone out.

The British Navy had designed them for other roles as well as planting mines on the sides of unsuspecting enemy ships. One other use was the cutting of underwater telephone cables at points along Japanese-held coastlines.

The assault on the *Takao* was carried out by midget XE3 under the command of Lieutenant Ian Fraser.

Towed from Borneo by the British submarine *Stygian*, in late July 1945, XE3 made her way into Johore Strait, where Lieutenant Fraser forced her under the very centre of the low-lying Japanese cruiser. Fraser's diver, Leading Seaman Magennis, left the midget, placed his charges on the *Takao's* plates and re-entered.

Another British midget, GE1, commanded by Lieutenant J. E. Smart, entered the Strait at the same time as XE3, after having been towed to the target area by the submarine *Spark*.

Both midgets successfully made their way out to sea again and were picked up by their escorting submarines without loss of life.

For his part in the operation Lieutenant Fraser was awarded the Victoria Cross and lived to write a book describing the action in which he had earned it. Leading Seaman Magennis was also awarded a Victoria Cross for his services in XE3.

6

Sunrise on 1 June 1942, revealed Captain Sasaki's five I-class submarines on the ocean surface south of Sydney Heads waiting for the midgets to return from their harbour mission.

With both seaplanes of his force out of action, Sasaki had no way of learning the outcome of the previous night's raid although his wireless operators picked up a Sydney broadcast announcing that two submarines had entered the harbour and sunk a ferry boat.

With the coming of daylight, Sasaki broke the pre-arranged formation of the waiting submarines and ordered them to disperse and submerge. When night came they reassembled and surfaced to wait again in the hope that at least one midget might return. In this fashion two nights passed in vain.

In the slight hope that some of the midget crews might have drifted ashore, Sasaki on the night of 2 June, ordered I-21 and I-22 to make a thorough search along the coast. At great risk to themselves the two submarines cruised close in shore, but there was no sign of the midgets or their crews.

Meanwhile an intensive aerial search was getting under way for what Australian naval authorities believed was a mother ship which had launched the midget submarines some 100 miles off the coast. It was at first thought that the midgets had delayed their attack to give the mother ship time to make a getaway.

Within a short time other theories about ocean-going submarines were also being considered. For several days while the search was in progress, the five lurking submarines were rarely more than forty miles from the Harbour Heads.

It was not long, however, before they were heard from again. On 3 June, I-24 torpedoed and sank the Scott Fell & Co. vessel *Iron Crown* with the loss of twelve lives.

One of the survivors from *Iron Crown*, Naval Gunner Cyril Sheraton of Hobart, described what happened to a *Sydney Daily Telegraph* reporter on 5 June 1942.

"I was in my pyjamas and watch coat beside my gun when the torpedo hit us.

"I tried to get my gun into action but didn't have a chance.

"I could then see the submarine about 200 yards away on the port side.

The ship sank in about four minutes.

"As the ship sank under me I was dragged on to a raft by Burchell and Hadfield. We were in the water from about 10.30 that night until 3.30 next morning.

"After the torpedo hit us the submarine came to the surface and circled us. We thought we might be machine-gunned so we lay still on the raft. The submarine finally left and we drifted on board the raft in the darkness."

Other survivors from the ship claimed that two submarines were at the scene of the sinking and that they had heard or seen a reconnaissance plane in the area.

Some men who were escaping in a lifeboat were followed by a submarine for about an hour. It came so close to them that Japanese officers could be clearly seen peering down at them from the conning tower. The men shouted and swore but the Japanese merely studied them for a while and finally closed the conning tower. The submarine then disappeared.

With dramatic effect, shortly before midnight on 7 June I-24 surfaced about six miles off the Heads and fired ten five-inch shells into Sydney before diving back to safety. The shells landed in Rose Bay, Woollahra, Bellevue Hill and Bondi, shattering windows and brick walls as well as causing a few minor craters in roads.

The only recorded casualties were one young woman, whose elbow was cut by shattered glass, and a man in a Rose Bay flat who broke an ankle jumping out of bed when an unexploded shell crashed through the wall of his bedroom.

At the same time I-21 surfaced off Newcastle. Firing flare shells first, she then landed a few high explosive shells in Parnell Park and into the harbour near a wharf. In neither raid was any serious damage done. Many of the shells fired even failed to explode.

On 9 June two of Sasaki's submarines chased and shelled the MV *Orestes* for some five hours before her speed finally shook them off. But on 11 June the Panamanian ship *Guatemala* was sunk forty miles north-east from Sydney.

While Captain Sasaki's 8th squadron of submarines skulked in the waters outside Sydney Heads events were taking shape in the north which were to spell disaster for the Japanese Navy in the Pacific.

On 5 May the Japanese High Command had instructed Admiral Yamamoto, Commander-in-Chief of the Japanese Combined Fleet, to take

Midway and the Aleutians.

The Battle of the Coral Sea, which had concluded three days later, upset Japanese hopes of occupying Port Moresby, but it did not greatly diminish the fighting strength of the Japanese Navy. Aware of this, American Intelligence gathered information from which they deduced that the next Japanese move would be against the Aleutians.

Accordingly an American force sailed north to intercept the expected Aleutians attack. The Japanese, however, evaded this force and landed successfully at Kiska and Attu in the western Aleutians.

At the same time, in anticipation of an attack against Midway, the Americans quickly concentrated near Midway a fleet consisting of aircraft carriers *Enterprise, Hornet* and *Yorktown*, seven heavy cruisers, a light cruiser, fourteen destroyers and twenty-five submarines. On Midway itself land-based aircraft were alerted.

Unaware of the trap awaiting them, a strong Japanese force of four carriers, two battleships, two cruisers and twelve destroyers, followed by support and occupation forces, began steaming towards Midway on 2 June. On the following day they were sighted several hundred miles south-west of Midway and were immediately engaged by land-based American aircraft. Next morning Japanese carrier-based planes raided the island and the waiting Americans, after locating the centre of concentration of the enemy fleet, unleashed an all-out air assault from their carriers and from Midway itself.

The battle lasted three days and when it was over the Japanese had lost their four carriers, a cruiser, a destroyer and about 250 aircraft. The Americans lost 150 aircraft and the carrier, *Yorktown*. For the Japanese the result was disastrous. They had joined the battle superior in carrier strength and still elated by their Pearl Harbour victory. In a matter of days the situation altered completely and the balance of naval strength in the Pacific was restored.

The battle marked a decisive point at which the Allies turned from defensive to offensive operations in the Pacific.

On 5 June 1942, five days after the midget submarine attack on Sydney, Japanese Headquarters announced: "On the night of 31st May, midget submarines of the Japanese Imperial Navy delivered force attacks on Sydney Harbour upon the east coast of Australia and penetrated deep into the harbour to damage one enemy man-of-war. The three midget submarines which took part in this attack have not yet returned."

Close on this announcement came news of the Midway disaster.

Towards the middle of June Captain Sasaki withdrew his 8th squadron north from the Sydney area. After leaving Australian waters nemesis overtook each of the five submarines, one by one. On Christmas Day 1942, I-22 was sunk off New Guinea by an American patrol boat. I-22's captain at the time was Commander Chinao Naruzawa, who had not long succeeded the former Commander Ageta on his return to Japan to teach at the Submarine Crew Training School.

On 27 July 1943, the American submarine *Scamp* sank I-24 south-east of the Admiralty Islands. The USS *Charrette* depth-charged and sank I-21 on 4February 1944 and eight days later I-27 went down under attacks by British destroyers *Paladin* and *Petard* south of the Maldives in the Indian Ocean. The last survivor of the Sydney Attack Group, I-29, was torpedoed and sunk by the American submarine *Sawfish* on 26 July 1944.

Only one of the group, I-21, had returned to Australian waters after the Sydney attacks. For a period in early 1943 she had operated off the New South Wales coast, claiming three ships and damaging two others.

Between 3 June 1942, and 16 June 1943, eighteen merchant ships and the hospital ship, *Centaur*, were sunk by Japanese submarines patrolling eastern Australian waters. The only other shipping loss was the *Robert J. Walker*, which was sunk by a German U-boat on 25 December 1944.

On 13 August 1942, the ashes of Lieutenant Chuma and Petty Officer Ohmori from I-27's midget, and Lieutenant Matsuo and Petty Officer Tsuzuku of I-22's midget were formally handed to Mr Tatsuo Kawai, then Japanese Minister in Australia, for return to Japan.

The ashes left Melbourne on an exchange ship carrying Japanese diplomats and civilians to Laurenco Marques in East Africa and there were transferred to the *Kamakura*, a Japanese exchange ship.

On 9 October the *Kamakura* arrived in Yorktown, where a young woman was waiting with the families of the dead midget submarine crews. She was the fiancee of Lieutenant Matsuo and she wrote:

Alas! You are now sad ashes
And yet why does my heart feel so happy
As though I could see you as in days gone by.

The young girl's dream of happiness was shattered and in her hands she held his ashes.

In Tokyo thousands of people lined the streets to pay tribute to the ashes of their naval heroes and a famous poet composed an ode commemorating their attack on Sydney. On Matsuo's first anniversary his mother wrote:

Strew the flowers, wind, I said,
It is for the sake of my son,
But my garden looks lonesome after the storm.

The heroic and honourable end of the midget submarine crews was not paralleled by the last voyage in store for the recovered midgets.

The attack, instead of striking fear into the hearts of the people of Sydney as intended, had only served to stiffen the public resolve to support moves for more vigorous retaliation.

A by-product of this resolve was a request from representative citizens and organisations in Sydney that the captured midget submarines be placed on public display and that funds, raised by viewers paying to see them, be devoted to patriotic purposes such as the Red Cross. The State President of the New South Wales Returned Soldiers Sailors and Airmen's League added his voice to the suggestions being made by asking that one of the submarines be placed in the Australian War Memorial in Canberra.

Finally, after the midgets had been examined by Naval engineers who were anxious to compare their findings with information gathered from the Pearl Harbour submarines, they were made available for public exhibition.

An ambitious cruise was arranged for the composite submarine, made up from the two damaged vessels. By the time it was over the midget travelled some two and a half thousand miles through the Australian bush.

Under the command of an Australian Lieutenant-Commander the midget was placed aboard army transports and began the first leg of its voyage to Wagga. One of the major obstacles on the cruise was the dubious capacity of country bridges to support the weight of the convoy — the bridge builders never having considered the possibility that their structures might one day have to support the weight of a submarine.

From Wagga through Holbrook the strange convoy proceeded to Melbourne and all along the route people turned out in droves to see the midget and contribute towards the patriotic fund. In most centres the arrival of the midget became the focal point for gala occasions complete with brass bands.

From Melbourne the submarine moved on through Portland towards

Adelaide and on several occasions Army Engineers had to be called upon to reinforce bridges over which the weighty midget had to pass. In addition to problems arising from having to pass over bridges, even greater obstacles were presented by some country overhead bridges under which the convoy had to pass. On such occasions the periscope needed to be completely withdrawn.

Although not commissioned as a unit of His Majesty's Australian Fleet the submarine flew the White Ensign from start to finish of the cruise. From Adelaide it travelled to Canberra via Ballarat, Bendigo, Albury and Gundagai and when it finally moved into the Capital it was flying a paying-off pennant.

On 28 April 1943, the remains of I-27 and I-22's midget submarines reached a place beside the Australian War Memorial in Canberra, and there, as one composite midget submarine, have remained since.

7

Naval experts in Australia were intensely interested in the midget submarines which had displayed so much daring yet achieved so little success for the amount of planning put into the attack. The same observation to a lesser degree could be applied to the Japanese Submarine Service as a whole.

Captain Ageta, commander of I-22 in the abortive Sydney Harbour raid and one of the very few survivors, said: "The Japanese Navy fought many hard battles but the most desperate were those fought by the submarine divisions. Our submarines went to battle one after another, never to return. One hundred and twenty-seven skilled and competent submarine captains, including my fifty-seven pupils at the submarine school, are now deep in the seas with their crews of over ten thousand."

The submarine service of any nation has always been one full of hazards and the history of the submarine itself has been studded with tragedies.

The first submarine to go into action was invented by David Bushnell, a Yale graduate who, in 1776, attempted to destroy ships of a British fleet off the New England coast. His attempt was unsuccessful and twenty-five years later another American, Robert Fulton, designed a submarine and offered it to the British and French Governments. His offer was rejected.

Although a number of semi-submarines were used with good results by the Confederate Navy during the American civil war, no significant development of the submarine occurred until the late 1880s when Nordenfelt, a Swedish inventor, designed a number of submarines, which he sold to Greece, Turkey, Russia and Germany.

The first British submarines went into commission in 1902 and, during World War I, both Britain and Germany pushed ahead with improved design and development.

Soon after World War I, there was a short vogue for large submarines and during this period the British built one displacing 2425 tons, the Americans one displacing 2730 tons, and the French one of 2880 tons. The Japanese concentrated on building large submarines.

When World War II broke out in 1939 the Germans had fifty-seven modern submarines in operation with others nearing completion. These soon became an even greater menace than earlier German submarines had been twenty years earlier.

During one phase of the war, after America joined the Allies in

December 1941, German submarines sank about 495 ships off the American east coast within six months. In the same period forty-two German and Italian submarines were lost.

Throughout World War II, 782 German submarines, excluding midgets, were destroyed out of a total of 1158 submarines and 700 midget submarines built between 1935 and the end of hostilities in Europe.

Japan, on the other hand, entered the war with sixty submarines but, by August 1945, she had lost 130 — virtually her entire underwater force.

For all their courage and training, the Japanese submarine divisions achieved poor results compared with those of their American and British counterparts. Whereas Allied submarines operated flexibly and offensively throughout the war, Japanese submarines, after the first year or so of aggressive action, were increasingly employed in supporting impossible situations or wasted on heroic spectaculars such as the midget attack on Sydney Harbour.

In mid-1942 the Japanese Navy decided to embark on widespread and large-scale submarine attacks on Allied shipping. The midget submarine assaults on Sydney and Diego Suarez were part of this overall plan.

On 7 August, however, American landings on Guadalcanal, Tulagi and Gavutu in the Solomon Islands, caused the Japanese to make hasty readjustments to schemes for disrupting Allied commerce and terrorising the shipping lanes. To cope with American counter-attacks they recalled most of their submarines from Australian waters and from the Indian and Pacific Oceans and concentrated them in the New Guinea area.

Growing American air and naval activity soon made it impossible for them to supply their beleaguered garrisons by normal surface transports. The only way they could maintain supplies of stores and ammunition was by using destroyers and submarines.

By November, the position of Japanese troops on Guadalcanal was becoming desperate and, apart from battle casualties, their numbers had been sadly reduced by malnutrition and disease and by shortage of food and war materials.

Submarines had already become their chief source of supply, but a Japanese Imperial command that troops on Guadalcanal were to be maintained at all costs meant that the submarine divisions were now to become primarily cargo carriers for trapped garrisons.

Most of the Japanese submarine captains protested against the passive role being forced upon them and argued that submarines would be wasted if their functions were reduced to the sole purpose of carrying rations.

Nevertheless, orders were issued by the Commander-in-Chief of the Combined Fleet, on 16 November 1942, and each submarine had one gun removed to make more room for cargo — leaving it with only two torpedo tubes for offensive action. Thus modified, Japanese submarines could carry about fifty tons inside and about twenty tons on deck.

Stores for Guadalcanal were loaded at Buin on Bougainville Island and each day a submarine made the hazardous supply trip. By January 1943, a few weeks before the Americans gained complete victory on Guadalcanal, some twenty Japanese submarines were engaged solely in ferrying ammunition and rations.

Towards the end of 1942, Japanese submarines were also carrying supplies to survivors of a Naval Landing Force stranded on Goodenough Island and to hard-pressed garrisons at Buna, Gona and Sananada on the north coast of Papua.

As subsequent New Guinea campaigns progressed, Japanese submarines continued to serve mainly as carriers of supplies. In the latter part of 1943 they were ferrying stores and ammunition from Rabaul to Lae and Finschhafen on the north New Guinea coast, still loyally but futilely serving a cause already lost.

Up to five submarines were engaged in this work and the average voyage from Rabaul to New Guinea was three days. Timing its arrival for darkness the laden submarine could come close to the shore and signal its presence by flashing a light through its periscope. The stores would then be quickly unloaded on to a lighter and the submarine would return to sea at top speed.

In 1944 the receding tide of war took with it the remaining Japanese submarines in Australian-New Guinea waters and, by the end of that year, the most desperate of all Japanese submarine units, the human torpedo, was in action.

In spite of the tremendous losses sustained by Japan's submarine divisions, the men who manned them went unflinchingly into whatever action the higher command ordained. Of 219 graduates from the 66th term at the Kure Naval College, eighty became naval airmen and fifty, including Matsuo and Chuma, turned to the midget submarine service. Most of them had entered the Naval College at the age of eighteen so that when the war ended those who survived were twenty-eight years old submarine captains or chiefs of the flying corps. Of the original course of 219 graduates, 119 died in action, mostly in submarines or in air battles.

In spite of this imposing record, few Japanese submarine exploits can compare in either audacity or results with some of those of British and German submarines.

One of the earliest and most dramatic incidents of World War II was the sneak attack on the Headquarters of the British Fleet at Scapa Flow, in October 1939, by a German submarine commanded by Captain Priehn. Inspired by the same fanatical desire to serve his country that drove Matsuo and his companions into Sydney Harbour, Captain Priehn sailed his U-boat through the mines and nets guarding Scapa Flow harbour. Priehn was determined not only to sink ships but to get safely away again.

Lining up the British battleship *Royal Oak* in his sights he fired his torpedoes and then dived, expecting to be immediately attacked by destroyers. When nothing happened after twenty minutes he surfaced and fired two more torpedoes in quick succession. As the *Royal Oak* blew up and sank, Priehn dived and wormed his way out through mines and nets to the open sea.

When he arrived back in Germany he was met by the Grand-Admiral of the German Fleet and a brass band. Then, after being promoted to Rear-Admiral and given the Iron Cross, he shook hands with Hitler.

Not long afterwards Lieutenant-Commander G. Phillips took the British submarine *Ursula* under minefields guarding the mouth of the Elbe and sighted a German heavy cruiser behind a protecting screen of six destroyers. *Ursula* dived under the destroyers and fired two torpedoes into the cruiser at such short range that the explosion shattered every electric light bulb in the submarine. Rising to the surface Phillips took a quick look at the wreckage from the sunken cruiser then dived and successfully escaped from the searching destroyers.

The important aspect common to both of these episodes is that the crews concerned survived to fight again. The tragic feature of most Japanese submarine actions of a similar nature was the loss of crews. These continuing losses of highly skilled men contributed in no small way to the almost complete disappearance of the Japanese submarine fleet as an effective force in the closing stages of World War II.

Captain Hankyu Sasaki, commander of the midget submarine raid on both Pearl Harbour and Sydney, said twenty years after the war: "When I started for the Pearl Harbour Attack and also the Sydney Harbour Attack commanding the submarines, Admiral Yamamoto said to me, 'Be sure to recover the crews.'

"Although I did my best, we could recover none of the crews in either case. I am very sorry for them. But those young men's spirit, fighting spirit of bravely carrying out their duty for their country even at the cost of their lives…that is something we should value highly forever.

"When Japan began to have a hard fight, thousands of young men devoted their lives to their country, with a belief in God's favourable wind in the sky and blessed reversal of their desperate battle by the Human torpedoes in the sea. It may fairly be said that those young men took over this spirit from those who started for the attacks on Pearl Harbour, Sydney or Diego Suarez, never to return.

"Apart from the outcome, what they did is quite significant. Their indomitable courage will help Japan spiritually to build up a peaceful country. And thus to try to keep the country good and peaceful will be the best way to console their spirits.

"I cannot help feeling great respect and deep gratitude to the Australians who courteously buried the young martyrs of the enemy with full Naval Honours and sent the ashes back to Japan. It was in the middle of the war, and their civil deed without partial feeling of friend or foe was really great and humane. It gave a good lesson to all the world what true humanity and reasonable sense should be."

THE END

Table of Contents